THERE'S LIGHT IN THE TUNNEL

COACH KEVIN KEARNS

To Danna,
Thanks for all the
support!
Best KK

Contents

DEDICATION

This book is dedicated to "Batgirl" and all the others that are becoming that...

Special thanks to Craig Rose, Lionel Beane, my sister, Stephen Whittier, Brian Fernie, Jamie Burke, Norman G, Dena B, McLean Hospital, the ECT people, Nick Peet, Kru Mark, Phil Healy, Jon Moll, Dr Yee, the yoga community in New England, Keith Foster, Ron Weinberg, Marcus Davis, Todd Hirshion, Sonny Romano, Jacqui Bonwell, Rolf Gates, Brian Hovey and all those others that I can not mention, plus all my current and past clients and all the fans of my articles and my work.

I do what I do to serve you all and make others better.
    Respectfully,
    KK.

INTRODUCTION

This is raw and this is real.

For people that love me, my loved ones, this is not going to be easy. It's going to be difficult.

It's going to be hard for me. As everybody knows, I'm fucking real, I pull no punches and this was my journey through getting divorce, the mess, the whole nine yards.

From selling the home, to having to get rid of everything and basically getting overwhelmed and falling into a deep hole.

My business fell down, my children were divided, money was a problem and I was basically starting from square one, trying to get back from being broke.

Trying to get out into the dating world at over 50, it wasn't so much fun, although I met some nice people. I also met some not so nice people and at my age, some people were like: 'Oh, go for over-30s, you can have all the sex you want.' Do you know what? That ain't what I'm into.

When you get to a certain age, it's never about notches on the bed post. I take a page from Woody Harrelson, from *Friends With Benefits* and that is that: 'It's not who you want to spend Friday night with. It's who you want to spend all day Saturday with.' I then add to that: 'It's about who you want to cook breakfast for on Sunday morning and then every Sunday morning after that.'

That's what it's about: finding that person that gets you and won't judge you, especially with this situation.

How do you have that conversation? 'Yeah, oh, by the way, I've got major depression and tried to commit suicide twice. On December 22, 2019, I tried to slit my throat and then four days later I tried to find a spot to jump off the Tobin Bridge.'

Um, yeah, wrong reel.

When I did the knife thing, I was like: 'What the fuck?'. I got sewed up after lying and making something up and then, you know, it just spirals.

I got overwhelmed. Everybody gets overwhelmed, especially with what's gone on with the pandemic over the past year-and-a-half, and we've gotten overwhelmed. Businesses have fallen down and all sorts of things are going on. They had me on a radio program back on April 1 and asked me what my major concerns were with COVID and the lockdowns. 'Depression and anxiety are going up, sobriety is going down and suicide going up' were what I said. I did miss out on the rise in domestic violence, divorce and child abuse.

We've got kids, aged eight to 11, who have suicidal thoughts.

Because I came out thanks to coach Steve Whittier, I saved 10 to 11 people in the past year from committing suicide and made sure they got the help they needed.

Like David Goggins said: 'Fuck it.'

You don't like me? I don't care, I honestly don't.

You don't want to follow me? Get off my page.

You don't like the fact I'm real? Tough. It is what it is.

So, my goal with this is to simply impart in everybody that it's hard and that it sucks.

The reason I named this book *There's Light In The Tunnel* is because if you're feeling depressed, feeling anxious or having suicidal thoughts, you don't want to think about the light at the end of the tunnel.

No, it doesn't work. You just want it to be over. It's almost like being in turbulence. You're like: 'Holy fuck, holy fuck, this sucks, we're going to die' and you just want it to be over, you want it to be done.

You just want it to be over. You don't want these thoughts. You don't even know where these thoughts come from. You feel worthless, useless, not like a man or a woman. Whatever it is, you know you feel unwanted, unloved, unsatisfactory, dysfunctional and that's not to mention the stigma of mental illness. I had that stigma, I was guilty of it.

'I can fix this, I'm coach Kearns', blah, blah, blah. Bullshit.

A friend of mine said to me: 'If you have a kidney problem, you go to a kidney doctor. If you have a heart problem, you go to a heart doctor. What makes you think you can fix the most complicated organ in your body? The computer.'

Find what works for you. For somebody that was working out for 42 years, exercise didn't work for me. I couldn't stand it and I remember the first time I went back to yoga class after three ECT treatments, going: 'Oh my God, I'm back. Oh my God, I'm back.'

Look at it this way, if you're in the throes of this, if you're in the shit storm and it sucks and you're miserable, it's okay, you will get through this. You are stronger than you think you are because if I can do it, you can too.

I'm a kid from Everett who grew up without a father from age 12, that sucked at every sport and was always picked last. I built myself up to the pinnacle, thought I'd married the right person — maybe it was for a while, and ended up not being — and then I fell down, right down, all the way down to the bottom, to the bottom of the pit.

It was like a scene from Sparta, that big deep hole, the abyss, the blackest of the blackest of the black pit. So, I know what the bottom looks like. That's what's great because they say that you know when you hit rock bottom and I hit it. And you know what? When you hit rock bottom, you fucking rebound. You rebound all the way up, you become stronger because you've just reinvented yourself.

That's right, I'm not Coach Kearns or Kevin Kearns 1.0, I'm Coach Kearns 2.50. Got it? And I'm relentless. I look at it this way:

I've managed my guilt about this, I've managed my shame about this daily, I've managed my regret about this and if it didn't happen, I wouldn't be able to talk about this and help who knows how many other people.

My goal with this is to help you. If my story helps you flick the switch to go and get help, to go and get ECT, to look at alternate therapy, to look at the carnivore diet and all that stuff, that's great, that's my intention.

This book makes $1 million? Great. I've got two kids that have got to go to college and I could use some money too.

So, this is my intro, this is my story. There are no punches pulled, it's raw, it's real and it's the way it is. Love it or hate it, I really don't care. I hope you enjoy it.

Be relentless.

Why?

Literally why?

I LOOK BACK at 42 years, going on 43 years, after my father died and it's a question I've asked myself a lot.

WHY?

WE ALL ASK IT. We want to rationalize what happened, we want to understand it, we want to figure out why.

WHY DID my father die when I was 12? It's a question that has perplexed me for years. He died to become who I am but by the same token, the dichotomy there is that he just died. It just happened. It is what it is, it's senseless, it doesn't make sense.

. . .

WE HAVE this need as human beings to rationalize it and sometimes you can't rationalize it. A man crashes a plane into towers. What's the rationalization behind that?

A client lost his son in an ATV accident last year and then he lost his wife a year later.

THE WHY IS EXTREMELY COMPLICATED. In fact, maybe it's not complicated. Maybe I'm incorrect, maybe it's not complicated, maybe it just is what it is and I think as a human being, that's the hardest part.

I KNOW it's a cliché and everyone hates it, but it is what it is.

PEOPLE DIE from disease every day, people get health problems, people lose their children and then what? You can become a widow or a widower. But when you lose a child, you're neither and that's the greatest fear of any parent: losing a child before their time.

A LOT OF TIMES, as to why, you just have to let it go. There is no why.

I COULD SIT and ask why my marriage went sour. 'Why didn't I do this better? Why didn't I do that better?'

WHEN YOU LOOK AT WHY, what ends up coming in is judgment.

WHY THAT HAPPENED, what could I have done differently? We attach judgment and it's just an experience and I know it sucks.

· · ·

YOU CAN SIT THERE and go: 'Well, if I'd stayed in this bad marriage for x number of years, maybe if I'd stayed in this job for x amount of time'… I don't want to sit there and say that. Do you?

SOMETIMES THERE IS NO WHY. To me, the only thing that's important is why do you want to do what you want to do.

I KNOW why I'm a coach, I know why I've been a coach, I know why I want to do what I do every day. I know why I get up every morning.

WHAT'S THE WHY.

MY JOB IS to try and empower people, to try to make them stronger and healthier, both internally and externally because when you get stronger and fitter you feel better about yourself.

IT'S the same thing with teaching martial arts, it's to empower them. It's always empowered me, from day one and sometimes when I push the envelope, people aren't ready.

THE CLIENT or the friend or whoever it is may not be ready for that technique or that level of what we're doing and it's unfortunate, it's a learning process. It's just like strength coaching. You've got clients that you may push a little too hard and it's challenging.

WHY IS A VERY hard word to figure out. It's almost like how. 'How did that happen?' It just happened.

· · ·

MY FATHER PASSED AWAY. It happens. I tried to commit suicide. It happens. Why?

I can add it up for days in my head, what went sour and what went wrong and what was going on in my brain but I just can't add up that day.

I JUST CAN'T, so why is very difficult. It's almost too judgmental for our soul. Why? Why did I do that? You just did it. Who knows. Trauma?

Why did I get angry? A trigger?

ONE OF THE best quotes I've ever heard was from somebody who said something along the lines of: 'Why can people push your buttons? Because they installed them.'

YOUR PARENTS, your spouse, why can they push your buttons? Because they installed them. And the why feeds into people all wanting to know why Robin Williams killed himself but we find out later that he had some disease.

I TRAINED a kid in his 20s, who was kind of like Forrest Gump. After a session one week, the owner of the venue that I was doing the class in told me that he committed suicide. I'm like: 'What?'

YOU CAN'T MAKE sense out of a senseless situation.

YOU CAN'T LIVE in fear of the why. It's like not taking a risk because you're afraid of getting hurt.

. . .

THERE ARE five or six thousand fatalities every day either in the US or across the globe in cars and it's like, if you don't want a fatality, don't drive.

IT'S LIKE COVID, right? I don't want to get COVID so I'm not coming out of the house for a year-and-a-half. I'm like, 'Fuck that, I'm going anyway'.

I PUT THE MASK ON, I was exposed to it, my mother died of it. I held her hand for 11 hours straight and she died of it.

I GOT TESTED the next day and I got tested the next month and I didn't have it. Are you going to live in fear?

I've been working on this for a year and then I decided to record it. I didn't want to do this. I didn't want to release my first book and people were like: 'Man, that's real,' because that's how I am.'

IT'S NOT all rainbows and sunshine out here, it's fucking tough. It's hard but it's rewarding at the same time.

MOMENTS MATTER. Those moments with your kids, your other loved ones, your significant others, those matter more than anything. Those are your personal individual retirement accounts.

IT'S like David Goggins says: if you've gone through something, write it down and put it in a jar and when you're having a rough moment, take it out.

. . .

NOW, take the opposite. Take another jar, write down a moment that really mattered to you at a certain point in your life, whoever or whatever it was, and put it in the jar so you know when you're feeling a little off — maybe you're not feeling good — you think: 'Hell, yeah, I remember that.'

WHY DO YOU KEEP A CARD? Why do you keep a love letter? Why do you keep your diplomas? To have that memory, to go back in time.

THAT'S one of the greatest gifts human beings can have, to go back in time to remember.

AT THE END of the day, the why... Why did the economy go bad? Why did my marriage go bad? Why did my dog die when he was only two years old? I don't know.

I HAD A DOG, Taz, he was two-and-a-half. My ex and I came home and we already had Flash the Jack Russell. We came home and he was dead. We tried to revive him the whole way to the emergency vet but his eyes were fixed and he was dead.

I FOUND out he had a heart condition. Is that going to make me sleep at night? No, he's still dead. And believe me, I've been there when you start looking at mistakes. If you make a mistake or you do something and then you want to go back and try to fix it.

WHY DID I DO THAT? You just did it.

· · ·

MAYBE IT'S A LEARNING PROCESS. You're fallible, not infallible. The only perfection is nature. The grass is going to grow, the rivers are going to flow, the sun's going to go up and the sun's going to go down. That's perfection but you can't be perfect, okay? There is no perfect.

THERE IS NO WHY. It just happened. It happened. Okay, how do I process it and how do I move forward? I think the hardest why is death. Why did this person die at a young age, why did this happen, why did that happen? They didn't deserve it, they didn't deserve to get cancer. No, they didn't. But sadly, it just happens.

WHY IS TOUGH. Why doesn't make sense and that's the hardest part.

I CAN'T FIGURE this shit out. I've been on this planet for 55 years. Put one foot in front of the other and just keep going forward to do the best you can do and then try to improve every day.

THE JOURNEY of a thousand miles starts with one step and life is a journey.

YOU MAKE mistakes and you make amends and then you have to move forward.

IMAGINE BEING 12 and your father dies and you look at yourself and ask why? What did I do wrong? Why did I do what I did wrong?

. . .

IT JUST HAPPENED.

WHY DID my kids move out? It happened. Why did one come back? I don't know.

We fall in love. Why?

THE WHY DOESN'T MATTER, it's the how, it's the qualities, it's who the person is. That's what matters.

THAT'S how I fell in love. That's how I got to a better place, that's how I got to a better job, that's how I got to a better space in my head.

YOU HAVE to figure out what your what is and what your why is.

I want this. I want to be a coach for as long as I can. That's my why. Why? Because I want to help people.

WHY DO you want to feel love? Because it feels good. Even when it's hard it still feels good. You know why? Because you know somebody else cares about you and that feels good.

WHEN YOU LOOK into somebody's eyes and you feel loved, you can't replace that with anything.

WHY DO THEY LOVE YOU? They can go through the reasons and it's just who you are. So, in senseless situations, with shit that goes sideways, it just happens. It's like going up in a plane and hitting turbulence. It doesn't matter whether you deserve it or not, it just happens.

. . .

WE'RE COMPLICATED, we're not loners, we fuck up and you've just got to keep going forward. The hardest thing with anything is letting go and moving on.

'I WAS in a bad marriage for 30-plus years'... Maybe it's just something you had to go through.

'I WAS in the wrong career for 10 years'... Maybe it's just something you had to go through to get to where you are now.

MAYBE IT'S a lesson you had to learn. Who knows what it was.

MY FATHER DIED to teach me the confidence to stand up for myself, to pull up my bootstraps. It taught me self-discipline, self-control, character, honor and to be the victor rather than the victim.

I TRY NOT to ask why I could sit there and say my cousin, Georgie, got a bullet to the brain from a bad drug deal two hours after Christmas when I was 15.

YOU CAN'T FIX the past. All you can do is make amends with other people in your life and move forward. Hopefully, they do too. You also have to forgive yourself because humans are always going to be hurt and wounded. It just happens. Saying otherwise is like saying you're never going to cut yourself shaving. It's like saying you're never going to burn yourself when you touch a hot pot.

. . .

WHY? It happens.

WHY DID it take me until I was seven or eight to have no training wheels on my bike? It happened. Why did it take me so long to tie my sneakers? It happened. Why was I afraid of heights? I don't know, it happened.

YOU CAN JUST GO on and on in your monkey mind, it just goes out of control. So, at the end of the day, the why does not really matter. How are you going to manage it and how, if you need to, are you going to make immense effects? That's the key. How will you learn from it? Take out the why and the what, that's more about your career and what you want from your life. Focus on the how. How do I manage this, how do I process this, how do I make it better, how do I fix this? Maybe sometimes you can't fix it. Maybe sometimes you have to listen to yourself and move on.

JUST THINK ABOUT THAT. Try to not make sense of a senseless situation? Eventually, let it go, put it down or maybe don't carry it as far or have somebody help you carry it. Look at it that way.

2

The how's

This chapter is going to be about my kids. It's going to be challenging and difficult.

My marriage ended. We were 30 years together and 23 years married and I didn't know just how unraveled I was going to get.

We were selling the family home but then she dumped the family home on me and I had to get rid of it myself, emptying out 30 years, 23 years of shit, the whole bit.

I knew the struggle the kids were going to have when I pulled the trigger on the divorce. I knew it was going to be harder on them than it was on me. My ex and I had agreed the night before that after we went through it, we would come to it as a team but she didn't do that.

I'm going to throw her underneath the bus right here because she looked at the kids and said that I had asked her for a divorce. I agreed, then said to her: 'You just fucked these kids up.'

I did what I had to do, I took care of my side of the street and by the same token I did the best I could with what I had. I had somebody going through alcoholism and someone going through recovery and for years I did the best that I could but I'm going to take full responsibility for how I fucked up my kids.

That being said, my kids got upset about something over a year-and-a-half ago — I don't know what — and a family member over-stepped their bounds and called my ex and told them something. My ex then used that as leverage to tell the kids that I was unwell and that they needed to leave, leaving the kids confused and me on the tumble down because my kids were gone.

My business was going sideways, I had just broken up with someone who I thought was the one after going through 40 other women. That doesn't mean I had sex with 40 different women, that's not who I am or what I wanted. These were, like, one-offs and three-offs.

You go with this person — oh, this looks kind of cool and then they ghost you or it goes on for three days and you think it's going somewhere but then they're a workaholic or an alcoholic. Or once they get the hooks, they're done.

For men, they get the hooks and that's it and there's women out there that just want the notches on the belt as well. I lied to myself on one occasion. The person drank too much and I looked the other way and it was stupid. But then again, how did I know until I went through it? The good news is that one of my mentors Kenny Lodato, one of my best friends, said to me that it's better to know after five months than it is to know after five years. That's why I said no, I told them that it didn't work and that I was out.

That person said that we were spending too much time together because we were seeing each other three or four times a week. She told me that she had been in a relationship before where she was seeing her partner once or twice a week.

'That's dating, that's not a relationship,' I said.

In your relationship, you need your space, you need your own time and that's fine. You have that conversation if you need space, you tell that person and you do it honestly. But by the same token, you want to spend as much time as you have left on this planet with that person. Just like your kids, you want to spend as much time on the planet with your kids as you can.

It's the same when you're in a relationship, you want to spend time with that person — not every hour but, you know what, a good portion of it. That's what marriage is, that's what a long-term relationship is. You share a bed, you share a home, and even if you're not sharing a home, you still want to be able to do it, you still want to be able to share that.

My kids and I had to let them go for 18 months. I reached out to them a few times and I did it by text just so they knew I was there. I got nasty emails from my ex and my youngest couldn't stand me for a while and now she's back with me and it was the fucking hardest thing I've ever done. That's truly where you let go and let God just let it go. You've got to give them space and giving people space is necessary. It hurts, it's not fun, it sucked every day, it sucked, I hated it not knowing if they were okay, if they were well, even though I was only seeing them half of the time. What's going on, how's school, how are their friends, who are they dating?

I'm extremely protective of my daughters because they're my daughters, and I'm extremely protective of anybody I love, male or female. Whether it's my best bro Steve Whittier, Nick Peet, whoever it is, they're my bros. Scopa, all those guys, they're my bros. Lionel Beane, Craig Rose, Keith Foster, Jamie Burke, Brian Fernie, you know, I'd stand in a fight with these guys.

My kids crushed me and then I learned something smart from somebody who ended up not becoming such a nice person. I sent them a card and then Chris Scabia taught me to send them a letter because they're going through the same thing. My buddy Mark Rossi kept telling me that they will come back, that they will figure it out and come back, but he told me that waiting sucks, especially when it comes to your kids, especially when you don't have the answers and sometimes — and this is a hard one — you can't make sense out of a senseless situation.

I don't know why, I really haven't asked my youngest but all I know is she's thriving, her grades are up, she's doing better, her weight is up, she's more relaxed here and, of course, my ex won't leave her alone, but I did. She told me to back off so I backed off but you sort of can't back off? It's hard.

'Get over it, you can't be controlling.'

It's like flying a plane. When the bumps come, you've kind of got to go: 'Okay, well, if I flew the plane, we would fucking crash' so I kind of let go.

It's their life. If she's late for work, that's on her. She gets fired? She'll figure it out. She drives too fast in the snow? She'll figure it out.

When my mother gave me the keys to the car, she didn't know if I was going to come back. You've got to trust them that they'll make the right decisions, that if you put in the right work and effort, that will help them to figure it out.

I remember the first time I saw the movie *Taken* with Liam Neeson and I remember practically ripping the seats apart because I was like 'Argh.' That happens with girls and women and daughters, shit goes sideways and it's unfortunate. It was the most challenging thing I have ever done since my father died. It was more challenging to just let them go, figure it out and hopefully they would come back. It sucked every day but as my therapist Norman said, it's a hole in your heart.

My eldest hasn't figured it out yet but it's a hole in the heart. Josiah just graduated and that's all good but it was a hole in my heart for 18 months. I know some people go longer but I'll tell you now that those 18 months, the ups and downs with me, the tears and fears and the whole nine yards, it was hard.

Some people had my back, a lot of people had my back and it's shit to talk about it and to be vulnerable about it with people and let it go. It would come up in yoga and I would just lose it. It's thinking about them: what are they doing, how are they? The whole nine yards. Yes, it was hard.

It was as hard as coming back from depression. Going through depression, the kids not being here and doing it on your own, figuring it out for yourself.

Sometimes you have to just be unbelievably patient with yourself and unbelievably patient with somebody else and realize sometimes it's not you, it isn't your fault, it just is what it is.

I know that's a cliche saying but it is what it is sometimes.

3

This shit hurts

What led to me attempting suicide was being overwhelmed and being overwhelmed was not understanding just how much everything was going to affect me.

MY GOOD FRIEND Keith Foster pointed that out. He alerted me to the fact that I thought I could handle everything when I couldn't.

I THOUGHT that going out dating, meeting new people, new women — this, that and the other — would help but it really didn't. It took my mind off it for a while. Took my mind off the death of the marriage, the knowing somebody 30 years and then getting fucking stabbed in the back.

I MEAN, it was coming. Fifteen years of complete crap, of bullshit. Fuck it, I'm going to talk about it.

The old saying of: 'You always hurt the one you love,' I don't know if it's true, but what I put up with for years was verbal abuse, it was manipulative abuse.

I'VE BEEN VERY quiet about it, I didn't want to talk about it and I didn't want to throw my ex under the bus but, you know what, it is what it is. I've already shed my tears and the thing that broke my back in the end was my kids getting upset about a *GoFundMe* I started because I made a mistake. It wasn't a bad mistake but I considered it a mistake because I started a page for my mother's nursing home expenses and I borrowed money from her account because I needed furniture because I was broke when I first moved out.

THAT BEING SAID, I didn't want to touch my retirement and I figured that if I borrowed $2500, I'd make it up with business and get that back but I didn't pay it right off.

MY MOTHER LEFT me $30,000 in bonds and I cashed them but I didn't manage the money correctly. I can beat myself up on that a little because, yes, I could have managed it better.

I THOUGHT I was in love with somebody who ended up being an alcoholic. After dating 30-plus women — one-offs and three-offs — I thought she was the next one and I was wrong. As my good friend and coach Kenny Lodato said: 'It's better to know now than know later. At least you forget it in five months.' That's true.

THE THING that absolutely broke my back was my business starting to slide. Things were going weird, exercise wasn't helping, nothing was helping and I didn't understand the level of pain I was in. Even driving through Norfolk, where I used to live, is painful. I have 19 years of memories there. When I married my ex, she was my best friend. We had our difficulties — we went through a lot of shit together and that builds relationships — and I think, at the end of the day, you can say you know somebody, but do you really know somebody?

I HAD faith and I had hope and I believed in the way I was raised by my parents. I tried everything. I've been in my own therapy for over 12 fucking years, marriage counseling three times, you name it, I tried it.

I WOULD SEE glimmers of hope and then it would just switch. Some of the stuff was just ridiculous.

MY WIFE and I hadn't been away in a couple of years and it was my 50th birthday and we hadn't had sex in four months and the therapist, right at the close of the session, said to my ex: 'You must be excited?'

MY EX REPLIED: 'I am excited, I am excited about getting away with them and I hope I like him again.'

I'M LIKE: 'Really, you hope you like me again? Why don't you just fucking punch me in the balls again? Why don't you just stick the fucking needle in my heart again. It's not a fucking pincushion, I'm still pulling needles out.

I'm going to fucking lay it all out there, fuck it and if you don't like it, I don't give a shit because it's about time I talked about it.

• • •

SHE'S GETTING her one-year sobriety pin, her chip. I'm in there, my neighbor — my ex's friend — is in there with me.

MY EX GETS UP THERE in front of 60 people, her sponsor's looking at me, giving me dirty looks and I'm like: 'Who the fuck are you, you fucking bitch? I'm with her every day and I'm watching the kids two nights a week so she can go to meetings that I don't know anything about.'

THEY BRING HER UP THERE, and she gets her chip — big, big deal. I understand that a one-year pin is a huge thing, I understand that it's a miracle that someone stays sober for a fucking year, it's a miracle, I get that.

MY EX SAYS: 'Oh, it's been an incredible year with lots of growth and blah, blah, blah,' and then she says: 'And I know I caused a lot of pain, especially to my husband.'

SHE WAS LOOKING straight at me and I fucking lost it. Five years of drinking, a year of sobriety and I lost it, just lost it.

FINALLY, you recognize what you did to me. Then she doesn't look at me for four days before we run into each other in the house and I was like: 'What the fuck?'

SHE SAID: 'Those weren't tears of joy?'

'TEARS OF JOY, are you fucking kidding me? Tears of fucking joy? What?'

. . .

I'M happy she's been sober for a year and I'm happy she finally recognizes the shit I've been through for fucking six years but this heart isn't a pincushion.

IT WAS ON AGAIN, it was off again and I remember trying to have a conversation one day — I can't remember what year it was — and I'm flying out to Buffalo to do seminars and certifications. I'm trying to talk to her about our marriage, trying to have a conversation and she's doing her nails. I'm like: 'Fuck this shit, I'll talk to you later.'

I BOLTED OUT of the house — I was two years sober — and I didn't text her when I landed, didn't call her other than to talk to the kids. I disappeared for three days.

FOR ALL HER FAILINGS, we did have good periods. I had glimmers of hope and then they would just be shot down.

I'LL GIVE you a really good example: in 2014, my book got made into a play and it was all the way in Connecticut. This book, my first book, all about my early life, talking about my father, the alcoholism, the bullying, everything, went on stage. It was tough enough writing it, imagine it going on fucking stage.

THEY THEN PUT me in the play. It was two hours away and she knew for six months that the play was going on. She could have easily changed her schedule but she didn't. The kids are excited, I'm nervous as fuck because I've never done this before in my life and they wanted me to go there for rehearsals.

. . .

I DON'T HAVE time for that, I have a business to run and a family to take care of. So we go down, I'm nervous as fuck, we get out there and I've only got two lines. I'm playing the instructor, there are 200 people in the audience and the play runs an hour-and-a-half. It's a two-hour drive and I've got to hang out a bit afterwards. It's Friday night, it plays two nights in a row and all proceeds go to autism.

ALL THE ACTORS WERE AUTISTIC.
    I went out there, it was the biggest accomplishment of my life and I got a standing ovation.

IT WAS two hours to get home, she knew that, she knew that for six months. She had to work Saturday and Sunday, double 12-hour shifts, she got the whole idea and could have easily changed her schedule and she fucking didn't.

THE KIDS WERE HIGH-FIVING ME: 'Dad, we're so proud of you.' I'm on cloud nine and she sees me right before bed and says: 'If I would have known how long it was going to be and how long it was going to last, I would never have fucking went.'

I GO: 'What? Why? Because we got in at about 11:30pm and she had to be in at seven for her shift?' She gets up at 2:30am though to do all of her self-care crap to keep her on level.
    We're in the therapists office one time and the therapist is talking about our qualities. I say 'Beautiful, caring'. You know, blah, blah, blah. She says: 'He's good with the kids, he's good at reinventing himself, he's a hard worker'.

. . .

THIS WAS a flip that started in 2005. We got married in 1994, 11 years into the marriage and yes, we had our ups and downs, difficulties, IVF with Emily. Emily had a heart condition that healed, Shannon had allergies that kind of got fixed. We went through all that bullshit and then there was just this bang. I'm pretty sure it started with the whole IVF thing.

I GET IT, we had two kids, back to back, and she had to have two C-sections and then ended up with two hernias. They had to be repaired and then that was it, it went downhill.

I'M SITTING HERE with a six-month-old and a two-and-a-half-year-old with an alcoholic and I'm like: 'What the fuck?'

ONE THING I learned from one of my old life coaches is that if you're starving, you'll eat garbage. I was starving so I ate garbage.

PEOPLE WILL SIT THERE and say: 'You're sensitive.' Fuck you, I'm sensitive. And you know what? I'm a human being and it hurts when the person you thought was your soul mate just continues to fucking stab you, not even punching you in the balls but stabbing you in the heart like a fucking needle cushion, like a pincushion.

YOU CAN ONLY TAKE SO MUCH, man, and then you fucking snap.

DO I SOUND ANGRY TODAY? Yeah, I'm fucking angry because of the bullshit I put up with and I'm still dealing with the same bullshit.

. . .

THAT'S MY MISTAKE, simple, I should have established boundaries, I should have put my fucking foot down. If the roles had been reversed and I was sleeping on the couch at 7pm or 8pm every night after drinking, I would have been thrown off.

DID she tell her father that she was in the AA? No, I dealt with it on my fucking own. Zero, zero help. The only thing I had was my friends. I couldn't go to her parents, they wouldn't talk to me. As a matter of fact, her father would rather see me dead, even though I gave him two grandkids and took care of his daughter for years with their own background bullshit. Everybody's got their own skeletons in the closet.

IMAGINE DEALING with that for 12 or 13 years. No wonder I tried to slit my own throat. Shit started falling apart, including my business. I didn't even know the level of pain I was in when I sold the family home.

IT ALL HAPPENED SO FAST.

SHE MOVED OUT BEFORE ME, and now I've got to clean up 19 years of shit myself, I've got to find myself a place to live and I've got to split the kids 50-50.

ONE OF MY daughters didn't even want to live with her and I was fielding phone calls constantly with her saying that she didn't want to live there and I was like: 'I can't do anything about it, what am I going to do?'

. . .

SHIT JUST KEPT UNRAVELING. Money was going down, I was living in 1100 square feet versus 3500 square feet, no neighbors around, no backyard, everything fucked with my head and then to top it off, I got behind with my mother's payments for her nursing home and didn't have any resources. I threw up a *GoFundMe* page, threw it out there for a day and my ex calls me because somebody in my family — and you know who you fucking are — called her and asked what I was doing.

SHE THEN ASKED what I was doing, convinced the kids that I wasn't well because the year before I'd spent some time in Norwood Hospital because of depression and the kids got nervous and moved out.

I BELIEVE in the 12 steps to keep you off drugs, to keep you off sex and whatever but I don't believe it works to fix a marriage, that's not what it's fucking for.

I PAID the price for a lot of shit. She wanted to become a yoga instructor. Three grand, I paid, anything to help her figure it out.

THERAPY, counseling, the whole nine yards. I found the marriage counsel. I tried it with one person and we couldn't afford it, I went back the second time with somebody else and didn't speak my piece and then the third time, I spoke my piece and she didn't like it.

SO, when I launched the *GoFundMe* page, my kids moved out. I still, to this day, don't know what it meant to them. I did find out, though, when my mother passed, that one of my family members reached out to my ex, stirred the pot and hit the hornets' nest.

. . .

I HAVE A CLOSE CLIENT, a friend, who lost his middle son at 22 six or seven months ago. I'm not trying to draw comparisons but I'm a few steps below him.

I HAVE NOT SEEN my kids intermittently. I just saw them 10 weeks ago when I moved. I've barely talked to them, my youngest can't stand me for some reason which I don't know. My kids, they have their own issues going on and they're at a vulnerable age. They're in their teens and I haven't seen them, it feels like somebody rips out my fucking heart every day. I have to compartmentalize that fucking shit daily. When I go into my client's office, it is the hardest feeling I have ever seen when he starts talking about his son. It kills me, it fucking kills me but I have to put it aside. It would be simpler if my ex and I got along but we don't. That hurts me.

I GOT OVERWHELMED, I got stressed out, this shit happened so fast, I wasn't eating, you name it,
It all fucking went sideways. I wasn't shitting right, I wasn't doing anything right. I was in so much pain, it was ridiculous and then all you want to do is fucking end it.

THAT'S all you want to do and the saying of: 'There's light at the end of the tunnel. You really don't want to think like that. That's why there's light in the tunnel.

I HAVE my moments from time to time where I'm really upset that I'm not
seeing my kids 50 per cent really upset. It fucking hurts. It's pain I can't even describe. It comes and goes.

. . .

24

YOU KNOW, I miss my kids. I was constantly involved in their lives. As much as I worked, as much as I busted my ass, as much as I traveled, I was always connected to my kids.

DO I feel guilty for trying to take my own life? Yeah, and I'm over it.

Will I hear why they're angry at me? Fine, let's talk about it because if I don't know why, I can't fix it.

THAT'S what I don't think is fair in life. Everybody gets overwhelmed and I thought I could handle it and I couldn't. If you're in that position, and you don't think you can handle it, get a therapist, call the hotline, whatever you're gonna do and don't think you're better off when you're not around.

That's fucking bullshit.

I THOUGHT that way and then I got a constant reminder of what I did to put me on the straight and narrow.

I'VE GOT plenty of friends, thank God. I have my friends and my sisters who have always had my back. My friends like Lionel and Craig, Steve, Scott O'Keefe. I couldn't understand it all and you know what, living in that house for six months, under the same roof, that was like the ultimate fucking torture every day.

SHE STOLE from the equity line twice when she was told not to. Shit like that went on and there was plenty of other stuff going on that I was unaware of.

SHOULD we talk about how somebody attacked the gas meter in the house too? Supposedly a rock. Yeah, right, okay, a rock? Sure.

My buddy Brian Ferny, who worked for the SAS, said: 'A rock's never hit that meter before and you've been there how many years?'

THAT'S FUCKING OBVIOUS, right?

NOT TO MENTION it's costing me over six figures for a 50-50 divorce without a judge. So, when I got my check from the house, from the sale, my half went to pay off the majority of my credit card and the other half went to my lawyer. Thank God my mother left me $30,000 in bonds or I would have been flat broke and still to this day she likes to poke the bear.

BUSINESS WENT SIDEWAYS because of COVID. She works in a field where she's all set and what did she do? Asked where her money was, the day after the fucking lockdown.

THANK God I have people in my life like my attorney who says: 'Look, hey, you're in some precedent right now, you're not making money, you're observing COVID, your business went down'. I told her I didn't have it right now. She broke my balls and gave me the option to pay for it over time, the whole three grand, even though she's making six figures-plus. She was constantly reminding me that I should be paying more child support, which is a fucking joke.

WHEN THEY LOOKED at our taxes, I made $10,000 more than her one year being self-employed but I got whacked and she wanted double.

WHAT ELSE? Trying to take my health care insurance away twice this year — yeah, how do you like that? Even though legally she has to pay for it. This is the shit I put up with. I'm just overwhelmed. You want to torture a parent? Fucking take their kids away. Now my kids chose and I have to be okay with that.

I'VE BEEN WORKING on this quote by Mark Twain for three years now and I've said it more than once. 'Forgiveness is the fragrance that is shared by the violet on the heel that has crushed it.'

I HAD TO FORGIVE MYSELF. Trying to commit suicide, was it self-centered? Yes, it is and it's the ultimate fucking pain.

YOU FEEL SO LOW, you feel so worthless, you feel so nothing. Then, when my kids moved out, I was like: 'I'm not even a father now?' That's when it just fucking crushed me. I was done, I was just done and then I just couldn't get out of my own way. Then I just fucking spiraled, I just kept spiraling. It just kept getting darker and darker and darker. Now I'm in a good place. Thank God for my friends who've helped me over the years.Over the past year, I've heard idiots say to me: 'If you want to kill yourself, you would have done it right.'

'DID you put it right to your throat? Did you pull it across…?' This isn't a fucking comparison, this isn't one-upping each other, this isn't a fucking contest.

I TRIED.

THIS ISN'T A DICK-MEASURING CONTEST, you fucking idiot.

· · ·

WHEN I STARTED DATING A WOMAN, somebody that I had known for a long time started calling me self-centered and I started questioning myself.

MAYBE I AM SELF-CENTERED.

THIS PERSON, who I've known for a long time, since high school, says: 'Oh, you're the most self- centered person I've ever met.'

REALLY, you want to say that to somebody who tried to commit suicide seven months ago, somebody that went to the Tobin Bridge to jump, that was in a lockdown unit on Christmas 2019?

KEEP that shit to yourself and if you think that, why have you known me for all these years and hung out with me?

ARE there any other underlying issues you have with me? Open your fucking mouth, bring it to fruition, if you have a problem.

HAVE I MADE MISTAKES? Yeah, everybody makes mistakes. Forgiveness is the hardest thing to do for somebody else and it's absolutely the hardest thing to do for yourself. We digest our failures. I've learned a lot about projection and there's a lot of projection in my former marriage, a lot of projection which I won't tolerate anymore. Now, I draw the line early and start seeing red flags.

DONE. Fucking over with. I don't have time for this and as my good friend's big dog John Johnson said years ago when he got divorced:

'You know, you can get comfortable being alone again.' And he's right.

THIS WHOLE CHAPTER is about being overwhelmed. I wanted to talk about this now because I'm feeling it now.

I THINK everybody has a form of PTSD out there. A good friend of mine, who will remain nameless, said to me that he had an amicable divorce and he still had to go to therapy. Mine was a shit show, it should have been a $20,000 divorce and ended up being over six figures.

THIS IS why I tell people that you're not too old to start over again. Fuck it, start over. Years ago, after my father died, after being sad for weeks, I figured out anger was easier than sadness and it is and sometimes you've got to let the sadness out. Nine times out of 10, though, the first thing I feel is anger. That's my protection mechanism.

WE'LL DO MORE to avoid pain than to gain pleasure. It's fucked up. Why do we do that? If you're out there, dating, in your 40s and 50s, fuck it, just keep going.

IF YOU FEEL OVERWHELMED, reach out to somebody. That's why I'm doing this, so I'm actually reaching out to you.

DO YOU KNOW WHAT SUCKS? The war sucks. Not seeing your kids sucks. Manipulation sucks. At the end of the day, stand your ground. Have your moment.

· · ·

BUT AT THE end of it, you have to compartmentalize shit, you have to put it aside because you've got to do your job. I've got clients to see, I've got an education to pay for, my kid's going to college, I owe money and that's fine. I pay my bills.

AT THE END of the day, when my kids come back, I'll own this. 'What do you want to talk about? I fucked up, I am sorry but I do mean it.'

I'VE ALREADY WRITTEN letters along the lines of: 'I am sorry, I fucked up. I got overwhelmed. Maybe I should have thrown your mother out.

'WE'RE HERE NOW SO how do we move forward? I never hit you, never yelled at you, never told you, you were wrong. I was always there, taught you how to ride a bike, drive a car, taught you how to swim.'

THANK GOD FOR MEMORIES.

HOPEFULLY, as they say, time heals all.

YEARS AGO, from dealing with other clients and going through divorces, and hearing the formula of two to three years to get back on your feet, it's taken me almost three years to get back on my fucking feet and a lot of people have helped me. I've helped myself, too, and I've had to make my own decisions.

· · ·

I HAD to bury my mother this year which was challenging and difficult, but I definitely have the support of my friends, my sister and my older niece. I hope to get to the point where I can be in the same room with my ex and we can tolerate each other but I don't know if it's ever going to happen. She made it messy, she made it bloody difficult and it was heartbreaking.

I'LL OWN MINE. I'll take all the heat from my side of it. When you can look in the mirror and say that you have tried everything, that's when you know you've tried everything.

THE FIRST WORDS out of her mouth when I pulled the trigger were: 'Is there somebody else?'

I LOOKED at her and said: 'Really, are you kidding me? Are you fucking kidding me? Really?'

I HAD plenty of opportunities on the road. I was not having any intimacy or sex at home. It's amazing when you think you have nothing in your 40s and your supposed best friend isn't even touching you, your love is not touching you but you have people 10 years younger at these fitness conferences hitting you up.

IT'S funny how you get degraded and you feel worthless and you don't feel attractive. You feel, I don't even know what the word is.

DID I SAY YES? No, not once. I didn't cheat once, that I can say honestly. I don't know if she can ever say that but I never did. I had plenty of opportunity and that's not to sound egotistical but I had plenty of opportunities. Those people are still friends, I've hung out with them, danced, had a good time, had a bunch of laughs with great memories and good people. That is what it is.

NOT TO MENTION that the divorce was put on me after agreeing we were going to come to it as a team.

I SPENT a lot of time at al anon [alcoholics' anonymous] and then I moved on. Because I was speaking my piece about some of the background stuff in my life and having a rough moment, a woman walked up to me and she said: 'People in al anon like you because you speak your piece.'

I DIDN'T PULL PUNCHES, I didn't hold back. I don't pull punches and people might get offended because I drop F-bombs or because I do this or that but I'm real, I'm not fake. I'm authentic and if you can't go with that then don't follow me, don't read my book, don't do anything with me.

I'M NOT GONNA BLOW smoke up your ass.

I WAS SHARING SOMETHING, past history, and a woman walked up to me and she said: 'I'd like to talk to you about what you shared.'

MOST OF THE time they gave me accolades, like: 'Wow, for a guy to speak like that…'

. . .

SO, I go over and I talk to her and she says: 'I think you dishonored your wife by bringing that up.' I looked at her and I did a double take.

I'm like: 'Excuse me? Now, if she was a guy, I would have fucking flattened her right there — you just said to me I dishonored my wife. Are you fucked?'

I WAS MESSED up for hours after that, I wanted to crack her upside the skull. My therapist was like 'Kevin...' and I was fucking pissed.

SHE WAS LIKE: 'Excuse me, you did more good than harm. That's her problem because it's something in her past...'

PEOPLE DON'T TALK about stuff and skeletons stay in the closet. 'Let's not talk about it, let's not break it up, let's protect the family.' Fuck that shit. Protect the family from what?

I DON'T HAVE anything against my mother for trying to protect me from my father dying by me not seeing him. You know what, Ma, I appreciate that you did that and you thought it was the right decision but it wasn't for me because it's been inside me for 40-odd years that I never said goodbye to my father.

THAT'S why I was goddamned sure that when my mother passed, I was gonna be with her every fucking second. There was no way I was leaving her side. I didn't get to do it with my father, I was going to do it with my mother. If I got the opportunity, I took it. If I got the opportunity, I took it. Was it hard? Yeah. Was it difficult? Yeah. And I was honored and privileged to be there with my mother the whole time, holding her hand. I made sure the priest came in and gave her everything that she wanted.

DEATH IS NOT EASY. I've been through it too many fucking times and I'm going to go through it more. From the ages of 12 to 21, I was at a funeral every fucking year. We had a big family. My father, uncle, and cousin George took a bullet in the head when he was 18 and I was 15. The list goes on and on and on.

DEATH IS NOT easy and everybody manages grief in a different way. It sucks and the way I look at it is that they're still with us. My father's with me every fucking day. That's why I wear his ring. My mother, I thank her for giving me my memories, for balancing bills and cheque books and

stuff like that, showing me how to be frugal and manipulate money and do this and that.

SHE HAD ALWAYS BEEN JUST like my Dad, they were both people persons. I can look back and say my kids learned self-defense. They learned how to protect themselves. They know enough — I'd like to teach them more, but they know enough to the point where they moved out and I'm confident that — as my good friend and yoga mentor Braxton Rose said — a baby bird can't fly in captivity. You've got to kick them out of the nest.'

BEING OVERWHELMED IS part of life, that's why you have friends. As an old client of mine, Nancy said to me one time: 'You can pick your friends, Kevin, but you can't pick your family.'

. . .

FOR SOME REASON, because they're connected to you by family, they think they have the right to open their fucking mouths. If you don't have anything good to do, say shut your fucking face.

MY ELDEST HAS JUST TURNED 18. I was hoping to see her on her birthday and I didn't. Did it bother me? Yeah, I fucking hated it. I don't like to use the word hate but I fucking hated it. I can't stand it. It sucks but I've got to live with it. I've got to deal with it and it's almost like somebody going through the addiction cycle and the recovery process and the whole nine yards.

MY YOUNGEST WAS PISSED at me, I don't know why and didn't want me to talk to her.

I'M NOT EVEN GOING to tell you the shit show I went through during the death of my mother. A lot of my close friends know. My ex was involved because my mother was at the hospital and she just started throwing gasoline on the fire, literally, on Christmas and the day afterwards.

I'M GOING to speak about that because it's the truth and I'm not trying to be right. I'm just telling the truth. I don't want to be right in terms of the truth, I want to be effective.

That was like totally kicking me while I'm down, hitting the fucking hornets' nest, poking the bear.

WHAT DID I DO? I just wrote it out. It's business now, that's all it is. She's probably still pissed that I was able to walk after 20, almost 30 years together and 23 years of marriage.

. . .

YOU CAN'T KEEP PUSHING people away and expect them to come back. Nope, doesn't work and that tug of war don't work for me. Either in or out. And then I waited — five years of drinking, six years of recovery to get supposedly to step eight which is to make amends.

WE'RE SITTING over lunch and she says: 'Just so you know, I'm sorry for everything I've done.' The good angel was like: 'Okay, she's trying' and the bad angel was like 'You're fucking kidding me, right?'

WHEN YOU MAKE AMENDS, you're supposed to walk through and acknowledge what you have done to them. It never happened to me. She was so proud of herself that she'd apologized.

AFTER FIVE YEARS of drinking and six years of recovery, that's all I got — sorry for everything? That's fucking it?

THAT'S NOT ENOUGH. You walk through it, you understand it and you feel what I felt. Words cut but actions speak louder than words.

WHAT I DID for years was unconditional love and I know marriage and relationships aren't simple, it's not 50-50 all the time, sometimes it's 90-10, 95-5.

MARRIAGE IS CHALLENGING, it's a constant state of compromise. It's what any relationship is. Any serious, intimate relationship is compromised.

. . .

SO BE careful when you get overwhelmed and if you do then reach out for help. I'm honored and privileged to help. I have helped at least seven or eight people in the past seven or eight months as far as trying to commit suicide, talking them out of it, getting them help and reading them the riot act. Sometimes wearing kid gloves and sometimes being a freaking drill sergeant: 'Get your shit together, go fucking get help. Stop talking about it and do something about it.'

HOPEFULLY MY RELATIONSHIP with my kids will be repaired over time but I don't know. Hope is an acronym — hold on, pain ends — so I can always have hope.

I TOLD them when they were 13 or 14 that they were going to make decisions in their lives as they get older. Those are their decisions, their choices and I told them that they would have to stand by whatever happens. If it goes sideways, they know to own it. If they don't own it, they move on, they move forward and do what they can but they will need to make decisions.

PEOPLE WILL SAY 'BE YOUNG, blah, blah, blah.'

HEY, I was young. I was 12 when I lost my father, then 13, then 14. Once I hit 18, I saw this pattern of drinking every weekend and I basically put the brakes on it because I was
    spending too much money and I stopped drinking because I saw a pattern and saw where it was heading. If I see a pattern, I stop it.

I WAS smart enough when I owned my gym. It was great for the first five years and then I got to the point where I'd had enough of it and I tried to sell it and it blew up in my face.

. . .

OKAY, failure. Big deal. I fucking moved on, I started a new company which went to *Burn With Kearns*.

I WAS smart enough that when shit went sideways with Kenny Florian [a then-UFC fighter], I jumped off the team two months before the BJ Penn fight, the championship fight. People thought I was nuts but nope, I had to do it. I trusted this.

OKAY, so when you're overwhelmed, sit down, evaluate, have your moment and then move on.

4

What can lead you down the
dark path

Ego. Let's talk about that and how I fell into the trap of the stigma that's attached to depression.

What I don't talk about a lot to a lot of people is the fact that I was in the hospital a year before this, before last year, for similar reasons. I went to Norwood Hospital for depression and I have to say that I didn't realize that I was guilty of the stigma of mental illness until my 15th or 16th visit to ECT therapy. That's when I realized, when one of the ECT people said to me that they deal with the stigma all the time. People shun. And when you think about it, people do shun mental illness all the time. I did it, I'm guilty of it.

It was my ego, that's why I didn't go and ask for help. Because I'm a master coach because I should be able to handle it and it shouldn't be a problem. I was under the impression that I needed to get over it, that it was all in my fucking head.

Ego is a dangerous thing and it took over my life. I'm adopted and people say: 'Did you have any hint of mental illness before?'

I'm like: 'No, man.'

And then I started thinking about it... In my 20s, I was dating somebody that wasn't the best fit for me but I was in love. We'd been together for a few years and then I started getting anxiety attacks, especially around food.

I would sit down, go eat and I couldn't eat and the only way I got myself out of it and actually reset the hard drive was to watch TV, watch parts of movies while I ate.

Then I reflect back to being, like, 10 and something happened. Maybe I suppress the memory, I don't know, but something happened where I didn't eat or take a shit for, like, a week. I went to the doctor and they gave me something and then I threw up and literally shitted my guts out right afterwards.

I don't know if I had it for a long time or not but in my personal opinion — they say remission — I say I'm cured and I say I'm cured because I made up my mind.

My Dad was a functional alcoholic. That doesn't mean he was a bad person but his ego got to him and he died at 48. He was told to take care of himself, not to eat crap, not to drink. He drank beer every day and that was acceptable but when you think about it, he died at 48.

I'm not even of the same genome and when I hit 48 it was the roughest year of my life. On that birthday, even though I'm adopted, I was like: 'Man, is something going to happen to me?'

I took a page from Dr Wayne Dyer and remembered ego stands for: 'Edging God Out.'

I broke when I was going through my depression. I was going into darker and darker places and nothing worked. No therapy, nothing worked and I fucked up. Yeah, man, I fucked up because I didn't go to one of my fundamentals. One of the fundamentals that I learned at 14 at United Studios of Self-Defense was that it's okay to ask for help and I didn't go do it. I didn't ask for help. I didn't go to my friends, nobody really knew much.

The night before or the day before I did this, Steve Whittier said to me later on in confidence when we talked about it a few weeks ago that: 'I knew something was going to happen the next day, I knew it.'

And somebody close to me said: 'If you wanted to kill yourself, you would have done it.'

When you watch the movies, it looks like that it's one quick cut and it's over but that's not true. I did it and then I thought about it and I was like: 'What the fuck? I've got two kids.'

Mind you, my kids had moved out for one reason or another, my business was falling apart and I dated somebody who I thought I was in love with, who wasn't the right fit. That fell apart and you don't realize, even if it's amicable, the affect that a divorce will have on you, physically, mentally and spiritually.

I didn't realize it and I'm not going to throw anyone underneath the bus but the last 12-15 years were rough. It's rough watching somebody you know go into recovery, the isms of our family disease.

I spoke to a friend of mine who got divorced — I hadn't spoken to him for a long, long time — six or seven months ago, and he was telling me that he still went to therapy for his divorce even though it was amicable.

It's just amazing what the ego can do to you and the weird thing is that when my father died, I had to kind of figure it out. My mother pushed me away when I was 13 because I kept going to her and because I didn't know what to do.

I just didn't know what to do and I had to stand on my own two feet, had to figure it out and martial arts and exercise became my go-to to manage my stress and anger. Yes, I was angry. Come on, read my first book *Always Picked Last*... I had anger, I was picked on constantly. I was the kid that sucked at every sport, the kid who last learned how to tie his laces on his sneakers, the last to take the training wheels off my bike. That's embarrassing, fucking embarrassing. And they don't let you live it down, they don't let you live it down at all.

A friend of mine who went through the same thing said to me: 'Kevin, how do you expect to fix the most complicated organ in your body?

'You have a gallbladder problem, you go to a gallbladder specialist. You have a kidney problem, you go to a kidney specialist.

'Your brain is the most complicated thing in the world.'

But, yeah, I just didn't get it. My ego got in the way and years ago I would think that suicide is the most selfish, self-centered thing you can do and it absolutely is. And by the same token, it's the deepest, darkest fucking place you could ever get into.

I'm lucky that I've personally saved six or seven people in the past few months because I put out a video on Facebook — thanks to coach Whittier.

I mean, I couldn't believe the benefit I got from ECT after just three sessions. The people at McLean Hospital couldn't believe the turnaround and thank God for people like Craig Rose and his wife Liz Rose who drove me to get ECT. It's a whole fucking day procedure.

You can't eat after 12. What did I do because I'm a nut? I got up early, went to work and I needed to eat to work but I put it to one side. I went to work for four or five hours and saw some clients. Bang. Craig picks me up and takes me to ECT. The whole thing, I thought, would only take a few hours and I thought I would eat and go back to work. You're not supposed to but that's what you have to do because you've got to pay the fucking bills.

Is that a little ego? Yeah, of course, but it's also what's necessary and I was chasing the green dollar. Why? Because money matters.

After 31 years in personal fitness training, group fitness training, certifications and all that stuff, I had been with a lot of clients who had gone through messy divorces. I'd heard the same thing over and over again, the same three-year timeline, that it would all be turned around after three years.

Do we speak to each other? No, but I've tried with the olive branch and it is what it is. It's difficult,

it's challenging and it sucks but I'm hoping that we can one day get to the spot where my ex and I

— after knowing each other 30 years — can actually be in the same room together.

It was challenging but my ego drove me into not getting help. I mean, what normal person wakes up at 4:30am to get in the shower and starts shaking uncontrollably for no reason? It just came out of nowhere. I had to cancel a client and I never canceled.

One of my clients used to call me the Nazi trainer. It was, like, 1995, my business was three years old and it was snowing every

Thursday in February. We've got, like, a foot of snow or more and she was like: 'Kevin, if you don't want to come, my driveway's not plowed, I don't think my street's positive...' So, I was there on time and she would call her friend and say: 'My trainer is a Nazi. He's coming in this weather...' And I absolutely would. I just don't quit, I can't quit.

It's like Joe Rogan says: 'The pros go to work. It doesn't matter if you're sick, you go to work.' That's me, I go to work. I've got to, I've got that work ethic. You know, we struggled. We had to do what we had to do.

My mother kept us together — I don't know how — with a family, a small job and everything else. You know, I just don't know how she did it, God rest her soul. Thank God she's with my father now.

Depression is a debilitating disease. You sit there and you worry about what people think about you, what they think about what you say, but then you realize — and I realized this from a friend — who your true friends are when you become fucking transparent.

I'm not saying that I have the same PTSD that military law enforcement officers have. But did I have a form of it? Abso-fuck-ing-lutely. PTSD is basically post-traumatic stress disorder.

Everybody deals with trauma differently. Everybody has a form of it and we all come across tragedy and trauma in our lives and go fucking sideways.

Life is not fair and it was never meant to be fair.

Ego is not simple, it's complicated. Kindsight vs. hindsight, take that right out of my vocabulary, because hindsight is all judgment. Shoulda, woulda, coulda. It's all bullshit.

How do you know what sharpness is until you cut yourself? How do you know what hot is until you burn yourself? How do you know what failure is until you fall flat on your face? How do you know what depression is until you're fucking depressed?

Nothing's working, nothing. Forget about taking a shit, forget about eating, forget about all of it, it's not working. Then you just want stuff to take up your time just to fill that gap so that you don't have to be alone with your fucking thoughts. Your thoughts are just so dark and so fucked up. To think about picking a knife up and doing it in your own kitchen, that's messed up.

ECT came at the right time for me because I was struggling to exercise. It made no sense. I would be going to yoga and hating every second of it instead of going off into La La Ville.

Exercise was my go-to. Now, you imagine having your go-to there one minute and then the next minute, it's not there, it's gone. It's like a death. That's the way my therapist, Norman, described it.

Divorce is the death of a marriage, death of a relationship and I know my part in it. There was a recovering alcoholic involved and I didn't establish boundaries. That's on me. Now, here's the story... Why didn't I establish boundaries? I was in love for a long time, I believed in my marriage, I believed it would turn around. I believed that addiction was a disease — like mental illness — but it was also a conscious choice to stop. You become what they call in remission and then it's a choice.

My therapist was like: 'You should have somebody monitoring you, a doctor, talking about medication...' I said that I wasn't doing any medication. I'd hit a point where, in August or September, I'd done so many treatments because I was on a taper for ECT. I was tapering every

six to eight weeks and then I spoke to the doctor who said that I was fine but that they would be there if I needed them.

I had more stress going into the ECT sessions and I now know the signs and symptoms.

If you knew the shit I went through after spending 11 hours watching my mother die on her 92nd birthday with all the bullshit going on. I had all the shit going on with my ex, family, everything and I still turned out alright.

Dr Mark Mincolla said to me that, after I'd given him a 10-minute synopsis of what had happened in my life in the past two years, if it was anybody else, they'd be dead and I'd take pride in that.

But all that shit, it gave me pause to reflect and really dig deep into me, to see who I am, to see what I want, to see what success is to me.

Isn't it fun that my kids aren't here 50 per cent of the time? Yep. They chose to leave for whatever reason. If it is what it is, they'll figure it out.

They're 18 and 16-and-a-half going on 17. I can't force it. It sucks and I have to compartmentalize it every fucking day. I hate it. Of course, my ex reminds me that I should be paying more child support because she has the kids full-time but that's not my problem. They chose that. My door's always open for them and I'll always be there for my kids.

I taught them how to ride bikes, I taught them how to wrestle, I taught them self-defense, I taught them kickboxing, I taught them how to swim, I taught them how to drive. I was very involved. As much as I worked, I was always involved with my two girls and nobody is ever going to take that away from me. No way.

Everybody knows. You ask my closest friends how much my kids mean to me.

I remember a former friend of mine, when I was a little vulnerable back in June or something, somebody I was dating who was just bad news. I remember them calling me selfish and self-centered and a bunch of other stuff and I said: 'Jeez, I wonder if that's true.'

You know, business was slow because of COVID and I called them. I couldn't get Lionel or Craig on the phone and I said to him: 'Just tell me.'

Out of nowhere, he told me that I was the most self-centered person that he had ever met. I hit the brakes.

I was like: 'I've known you over 30 years.'

Is that a reflection of him? Probably. But do you really want to be telling that to someone who's just tried to commit suicide seven months earlier? Is that empathetic? Is that thoughtful and kind? I don't think so.

Ego again. That's where ego eats in. Why did he say it? Right, I haven't spoken to him since... I don't need that shit in my life.

I'm 55, I feel like I'm 35. That's fine. I don't need the grief, I don't need the bullshit, I don't need any of this.

You want to judge me? Be careful pointing the finger because you've got three more pointing back at you.

You want to judge me? Judge yourself.

I have goals, I have certain things that I have to achieve and I have to get there. It's a must, as Anthony Robbins would say, a must. I'm on a mission. My mission when I first graduated from

college was to help end obesity one step, one person at a time. Now, I realize that obesity has similarities with alcoholism and drug abuse.

Obesity and overeating is connected to depression. Look what's going on now, we're social animals, we need a connection. It's all in your head, it's a chemical imbalance, it's fucked.

When you pick up the knife and do it and then you sit there and you're bleeding, you go: 'Why did I do that?'

Well, I did it because I was in the blackest of black holes.

When I was going through all the messy shit, trying to keep my marriage together, I was being told that there was light in the tunnel but you can't think like that when you're depressed. You can't think at all when you're depressed, when you're anxious, you just want it to end. You want to know there's light at the end of the tunnel. You want to know that there's hope, with hope being an acronym for hold on, pain ends.

Light at the end of the tunnel… You're like: 'What, I have to go some place else?'

No, people that are in that situation, they need hope now, they need light now. It's dark, man. You're in a pit and you just keep sinking and sinking. You try to claw your way out of it, you just want it to stop. That's right, you just want it to end, to be over with. That's why you think about suicide because you just want to be out of the pain you're in. You're in so much pain that you don't know how to get out of it, you don't know how to do anything with it, that's how much pain you're in. It's not even measurable.

If the doctor asked you your pain level, you wouldn't even be able to describe it. That's how much pain you're in.

It would come and go, come and go and the best time for you was when you were sleeping. Even that wasn't gracious but the rest of the time it sucked.

I was bullshitting the whole time, in front of clients and I had to put on a fake face for people who saw me as tough because I wear my heart on my sleeve. Some people think that's a bad thing but I don't give a fuck. Go and fuck yourself.

I've also been called too sensitive but I don't care because that makes me a good coach.

I'm not trying to be right, I want to be effective and tell the truth. That's all I care about. This whole being is the right thing, it's all about ego. None of that matters. Truth matters, though. Tell the truth, have integrity, honor, character and compassion.

Check your ego at the door. Why is it important? What do you want out of it? What do you want out of life? I know what I want.

I'm not going to retire. Please. Me? What am I going to do, play golf? I'm not going to play golf.

Looking back, I've spent 30 years in this business. Everything goes sideways and I've failed plenty of times but I'm cranking away, making money, doing well. I bought a health club, it's the happiest day of my life. I have the second happiest day of my life when I sell it.

9/11 hits, crushes us and the bottom falls out and I was an absentee owner for five years. Boom. That blows up and I reinvent it with Burn With Kearns. That cranks out, I get involved in UFC, start doing my own DVDs and boom, that falls.

You fall down, you get back up. You fall down, you get back up. Nobody owes you shit. You do it for yourself.

You can't quit when you're depressed, even though all you can think about when you're depressed is quitting and the pain ending.

I can't even describe the level of pain. You just go into a deep, dark place and, in some cases, put a knife to your throat and attempt suicide. It's irrational.

I look back now at what I did and it makes no sense. Everybody has some level of depression.

Somebody said to me: 'Oh, if you don't have the money to write the book, why don't you wait…' No, the book's needed now, I need to write it now. Not just for me but for other people.

I put up one little thing about feeling better after three ECT treatments and talked about my depression and the whole nine yards and I got 1500 to two thousand views in one day from that video. I had people from high school reaching out to me and that was back then when the economy was fine, when everything was great and when there was no COVID.

Don't be afraid to talk to somebody, don't be afraid to call up the hotline, to put your ego aside and ask for help. Realize that you're not fucking alone.

Listen to this: you need me, you fucking call me.

Don't hide. My friends that have gone through this, I've called them out.

One thing I want this book to do is to make a difference, to let people know that they're not alone.

Nobody should go through that, man. Nobody. It's like a cement overcoat that you can't get rid of. It's just weighing you down and that's why it drives me insane when people don't pump other people up.

Actions speak louder than words, yes, but words cut, man, and they matter. You don't say something to someone and then fucking trash them.

Look beyond the cover, look at what's inside of people and everybody has a fucking gift. Don't keep your gift wrapped.

Get rid of the negativity. Write it all off because you're just filling your head with the wrong thing and then reach out to your solid friends, your friends who check in on you and who say: 'Hey, come on, get up. I'm going to be there for you.'

You need a friend who will tell everybody to back the fuck off, the friend who will take your hand and tell you that you ain't going to quit today.

You want a friend who'll say: 'Give me your hand, I'll pull you up'. A friend who won't care how heavy the load is. You reach for them, you pull them up.

You can pick your friends but you can't pick your family. That said, the right friends become your family.

Your friends don't judge you and if they do then they don't belong in your friendship circle.

48

I can name at least 30 close friends of mine that will be there for me and I'll be there for them because that's the way it is.

I'll lay down in traffic for them because that's the way we roll in Boston.

I give back. Sometimes, I'll walk into yoga and ask them to put somebody on my account today. Or I'll go to Starbucks and buy a $25 gift card and give it to someone. I try to make someone's day with a random act of kindness. It not only affects the serotonin levels of the person receiving, it affects those around them and also affects the person giving. It's a ripple effect.

Life is up and down. The problem is that when you're in that depression, it's down, down, down. It's like a cellar, it just keeps going and going and going. Anxiety is the same. You just think: 'When is it going to end?'

Take time to reflect, take time for yourself and reach out to the people that care about you. Worst case scenario, reach out to a hotline. Reach out to a hotline. It's not your fault that you feel this way.

Something happened and you chemically got all fucked up. Whatever it is, that's what happens. 'It's not my fault, I can get better, I'm not alone.'

You're not alone. Remember that. You're not alone. I care about you, other people care about you and if everybody's gonna do this then it's just a reflection of themselves. You will get better, you will move forward and you will become successful, whatever success is to you.

Success isn't just measured by your house, your cars, your money, that isn't success. What are you doing for others? What are you doing for yourself? How do you give back? How do you make somebody feel good?

You never know what you're going to hear or what you're going to say that's going to help somebody else and vice versa.

When something speaks to you, do it.

But you know what? Always be a white belt. Progress is not perfection. Say that to yourself.

If you want to do something funky, something different, the likelihood is that you're going to get people criticizing you but it'll help you get out of the funk.

I did ECT and I had a doctor client rip me apart for it. I had to tell him to shut up because it worked for me and because it will be there for me if I need it again. I won't need it again though and that's all because I made up my mind.

I fixed myself, and you can fix yourself too. Push the ego aside, reach out to your real friends, ask for help, be transparent and you'll get there. Those are the foundations. Hold your vision, keep your passion and maintain and invest in perseverance, no matter what the fuck anybody says.

5

Time is irrelevant

We have experiences and then we attach meaning to them. It's bad, it's good. The other thing we attach to our experiences is time. 'Jesus, it shouldn't have taken me that much time'.

How do we even know that? Time is irrelevant.

Leo Tolstoy was on his deathbed talking about having an illness, talking about how much he hated his life, hated his wife and he said: 'At the end of the day, my whole life was wrong.' He croaked.

I don't want to go out like that. Do you? No fucking way. I ain't going out like that.

Feelings are just information. It's how we interpret those feelings. Then we attach meaning to them. 'I'm scared, what's wrong with me?' Nothing is wrong, you're just scared. You're on a plane, there's turbulence, I'd be shitting my pants too.

'I feel uncomfortable...' Okay, life begins at the end of your comfort zone. Sometimes every fall from grace brings you higher.

People think that they're not going to struggle, but if you look at any entrepreneur — anyone who has made it in the eyes of society — they've struggled. I did. I still do and we all struggle.

When you get to the prince level, it becomes irrelevant. You've got people wiping your ass and shit so it becomes irrelevant. You're not in touch with real people, you're not in touch with reality.

The reality is that you get up in the morning and you go to pee, you wipe your own ass and you go to work. Whatever that work is — hopefully it's something that inspires you — something you love doing on a regular basis because otherwise you're just spinning your wheels. That's okay for some people though and there's nothing really wrong with it.

As my father used to say to me, God rests his soul, there's not one unimportant person in the world. You can learn something from the garbagemen, to the postman to the tax accountant. It doesn't matter.

There's a big concept out there called emotional intelligence. IQ is great but being smart doesn't mean you know how to interact with people. Being smart doesn't give you sensitivity to being able to read people or understand what they're thinking. People say 80 per cent of things with their body language.

Look at grading in schools. Grading in schools is ridiculous. They have 'A, B, C, D,' and then they miss an 'E' and have 'F' because you failed. My youngest daughter just went through this. She had to make up a quiz and the teacher wouldn't let her and she was failing history.

I'm like: 'What kid didn't drop their grades this year with all that's going on? We haven't been through a pandemic since the Spanish flu.'

What if everything that happened now happened in the 80s and 90s before the internet. What were the kids going to do? They probably would have still gone to school. Nowadays we have the internet to fall back on and we can do everything mobile.

It's funny that with all these masks on and everything else, people don't want to interact anymore. It's all just stories that we tell ourselves.

I remember when everybody went back to school for a short time, and somebody coughed in class and they sent the whole classroom back. I'm like: 'Really?

My mom passed away on her 92nd birthday. She passed away

on December 24, 2020, due to complications with COVID but the way I see it, if you live to an age where you see your kids get married and have children, then you've lived a full life.

The last seven years, she wasn't happy, she was in a nursing home. I ain't going out that way, I ain't going to no fucking nursing home. That ain't going to happen for me. I'll probably go down doing push-ups and then croak.

Be careful with the stories that you tell yourself.

I remember sitting at the Idea Fitness World Trade Show, and they brought me out for a session they were filming called Train Like An Ultimate MMA Fighter. The place was packed.

There was probably 200 people. There was a 5000 square feet area and I had to do a PowerPoint which I hate. I need to get over that but it's hard for me. I just want to train.

Touch it, smell it, taste it, eat it. I'm a hands-on type of guy and I've always been like that. That's probably the martial artist in me but I've always been like that. I can't learn martial arts in a book, it doesn't work. So, I turned around and was cracking jokes. Nobody was laughing and I started to get insecure and worried that they were judging me. But who cares if they're judging you? At the end of the day, they came to see you.

Something was snapping at me and I just went 'Fuck it.' I swung for the fences. I just made it entertaining and it just took off. Why? Because I let go of the stories.

It's like when people rip you down on social media, you want to fight back, but as David Goggins says: 'Fuck people.'

'When people are telling you to relax because you're jacked up, they're just hiding how jacked up they are.'

We're all jacked up. We've all had trauma, we've all had experiences, we all tell ourselves stories. I think fear's a good thing because it tells you something that you need to get over.

It's like being on a bumpy flight and you tell yourself you're going to die. Is that reality? No. At the end of the day, it's one of the safest ways, if not the safest way, to travel. Those pilots are over-trained. We give a license to somebody that's been on the road for six months with a 2500- pound weapon to drive around on highways.

The only way to keep yourself from getting in an accident and not getting killed driving is not to drive. What's that about? Why not experience life? If they can pull the Star Trek shit off and they can beam you here, there and everywhere — versus taking, like, 1500 hours to get to Australia — I'm all for it, man, just because of time.

It really is a matter of just letting go and I work on this every day. Letting go of the stories, letting go of the bullshit, letting go of what somebody told you. Those are just stories, they're just labels that somebody put on somebody else. It is what it is, let's move forward.

The big takeaway from this chapter is to let go of the stories.

One of my first therapists, Dina Brubeck, said that yoga was a great metaphor for life. It puts you in an uncomfortable position. And believe me, when it's 95 degrees and you're in a chair and you're rotating and you feel like your intestines are about to come out and the teacher is like: 'Breathe, be one with it.' Then you go: 'What's this all about?'

Sometimes people are ahead of me in the poses at practice but I don't care. If I'm sitting in a tree pose or warrior two longer than anybody else, I really don't give a fuck. It's my experience, not theirs. I don't care what they think. Who gives a shit. If I like it and it feels good, I'm going to leave it there.

It's hard when you're out there and you're in videos and you've written articles and you've got all this other shit going on. As Goggins said: 'The more successful you become, the more haters you're going to have. If you can walk on water, the haters are going to tell you that the reason you can walk on water is because you can't swim.' They're going to see the negative.

No, I can just walk on water. You've got to always be a white belt, always keep learning. The more you think you know, the less you know. Let go of the bullshit of every day, whatever story that is.

Before civilization and home life and school life and everything else, there was no timeframe, there was no breakfast, lunch and dinner. You just ate when you were hungry. Me? I'll eat breakfast anywhere between 4am and 8am and I'll eat lunch anywhere from 11am to 4pm, depending on when I'm hungry. I'll eat dinner anywhere from 6pm to 10pm at night. Big fucking deal. I listen to my body and I eat when I'm hungry.

At the end of the day, it's okay to cheat. I love coconut milk and ice cream sandwiches and they're only 100 calories a piece. Do I count calories? No. I eat when I'm hungry, I eat when I want.

Am I smart enough? Yes. I'm disciplined enough not to eat shit all the time. I don't drink soda — that's your number one killer right there — I don't smoke, I do drink alcohol but I don't drink to excess. I train at least five to eight hours a week, sometimes two a day. I definitely try to take one day off if not two and there are other days when I'm going to tell myself a story. But then there are times when I feel so good, I feel so in the moment, that I just have to keep going.

At the end of my workout today, I was doing car pushes because I felt good. But we have to be careful of the stories that we tell ourselves and we tell other people.

You've got two ears and one mouth for a reason and it was once said that when you meet somebody, you need to be careful not to prepare a speech instead of listening. That includes listening to yourself.

Your heart knows intuitively. Your heart is like your second brain. It's like when you meet someone and you fall in love. It's love at first sight. It does happen.

I love the quote from Dr. Wayne Dyer about not failing. 'You just produced results you didn't expect.'

It's like dealing with divorce. Yeah, it's a failure of a relationship, it's a failure of a marriage, of a partnership but at the end of the day, you're just refining what you want.

It's a matter of letting go and not judging because fuck it, who cares? Who cares at the end of the day? Let's just be human. As an entrepreneur for 34 years, I have a hard time tapping the brakes but when I shift into neutral, I'm in neutral.

You've got to be. One minute, I can train with a UFC fighter and the next minute I can be training with my 86-year-old customers who just doesn't want to fall down. I can't be all hyped up or all crazy.

The big message here for this chapter is to learn to let go.

I went to Starbucks today to do some work and it was just too busy for me, just too fucking busy. There's nothing wrong with goals because when you commit to goals, you also learn to let go. It's right place, the right time for everything and you just have to let go, be you, do you and forget about everybody else.

Just be, it's okay. Who cares what society says and what everybody says? Fuck them. Do your thing and do you, the best you can.

6

The stigma of mental illness

I didn't realize that one of the things attached to mental illness was a stigma. 'It's in your head, suck it up…'

When you think about it, I have friends like Richie O'Connor who have PTSD who did seven tours of Afghanistan. How can you not? You're told to go and kill people and shitloads of your friends die.

One thing Keith Foster, a friend of mine from Ireland who I'm dedicating this chapter to said to me which made a lot of sense is that I was overwhelmed. I didn't get that.

It was three months into ECT, where the IV ninja — I wish I remembered her name — explained to me how much they have to deal with the stigma every day, helping people and dealing with people with mental illness.

That's the big thing, it's the last word: illness. If I said cancer instead of mental illness people's reactions would be different. I had a lot of clients who were aware of what was going on when I was faking it until I made it and they just stuck with me. When you're in that mindset, you just want shit to take up your time.

Depression, anxiety, mental illness, PTSD and all that stuff, it overrules your life and you literally get overwhelmed. It affects your digestion, it affects your bowel movements, it affects your sexuality, erections, eating, training, sleeping. It fucks up your whole life and you can't get rid of it. It weighs you down. You're carrying it from place to place and it fucking sucks.

Normally, exercise is my go-to and has been since I was 13 when I discovered martial arts. I train like an animal every day. I've had 28-year-old fighters try to train with me and I bury their asses because I'm not right in the head — and don't take that the wrong way.

If you read my first book, *Always Picked Last*, I sucked at everything. What ended up happening is that my brain processes the word can't and says: 'You can't tell me that.'

I don't quit. That's what got into me and that was the problem with being overwhelmed. I was completely guilty of having that stigma and at times my ego took over. I try my best to be as humble as possible but sometimes I'm not.

'I'm Coach Kearns, I can deal with this. I've written all these articles and trained all these fighters and I have an international brand.' Yeah, shut the fuck up, Kevin.

I remember making the comeback, going to my first yoga class and I didn't even know it was over. I was in such a state of joy and was like: 'Okay, I'm back' and that was about a week after being in hospital.

That was all thanks to my good friend Steve Whittier, my business coach, who wanted me to launch a seven-day campaign that we marketed organically. We wanted to talk about something tough.

I didn't talk about my twice-attempted suicide but I did talk about my depression. I came out with it and was very open, very raw and real and I got 1500 hits on social media in one day.

That was powerful. But until Keith Foster told me I was overwhelmed, I never understood what that meant.

I tried to keep my marriage together. I got divorced. Somebody attacked my house and gas meter. I sold the house. I was 50-50 with the kids.

I moved out of my 19-year neighborhood and moved into a box apartment. The divorce cost me

$100,000 and my business started to slide.

Then you have to start all over again. You think that's what I want? You just want to know that the person you were married to had your back.

You want to be with the person who you feel comfortable with, the person who makes you feel real love, not fake.

The person you thought was the one, they weren't the one. They burned you, they lied to you, they did the wrong thing by you. It's overwhelming and it all fucks with your head.

People say they know me. My response is always: 'What? You do? Because you've known me 30 years?'

I had a friend who I'd known for 25 years who, about a month ago, had just dropped me off a cliff. 'Are you not going to tell me why?'

This person spent time at my house every holiday because they lived in a different state.

In divorce, you can be happy but it's a dichotomy because at the same time you're sad because it's the death of a relationship, the death of a marriage. As bad as it was, it sucks and that's overwhelming.

My older daughter had difficulties with the 50-50 and there was all kinds of other stress.

One of the first things that goes sideways when a relationship or a marriage is heading for divorce is intimacy. Physical and emotional intimacy goes out of the window. You can forget about the sex. Communication goes out of the window.

Sex is a complete vulnerability, complete intimacy and complete trust. That can be overwhelming and trying to restart that with somebody, plus trying to move on with your life while battling with everything, is overwhelming.

And here's the key: It's okay to be overwhelmed. That's why you go to therapy, that's why you look at other activities, that's why you look at different things and, ultimately, that's why I went to ECT. I had to do something different. Alcoholism and drug abuse is an addiction. It's a disease but it's also a choice. You have a choice to stop it.

You can be cured or fixed or whatever you want to call it. That's a choice, to get help and you need to forgive yourself because it's not your fault, it just happened.

You can't blame yourself for getting cancer unless you're smoking but plenty of people get cancer who don't smoke. And then if you're lucky enough, down the line, you'll hopefully meet the person who you think: 'There they are'. When you look over your shoulder and you say: 'Yep they got my back.'

You might have to take a knee. Maybe you have to take two knees after you've raised your kids and you've worked your ass off and the whole nine yards but at some point you have to go back to battle.

However, you want that someone who'll stand with you in battle, the one who'll cover the angles while you take your minute.

You can go to your friends, you can bitch and moan and they can tell you this, that and the other, but at the end of the day, you're still alone.

I've been fortunate enough that since I came out, I've saved probably 10 people from committing suicide, all because I came forward. But when I miss the mark, when somebody doesn't reach out or I didn't come out quickly enough, it sucks, it fucking pisses me off, it drives me nuts because it's another life lost.

I've heard of 11-year-olds committing suicide, I've got a client whose 12-year-old daughter is cutting herself because the Dad is a manipulative fuck.

As David Goggins said: 'Fuck people.'

After age 30, you've had trauma. My trauma started at 12. I buried my father when I was 12 years old. Do you want to see your father in a coffin at 12 years old for five days straight, three times a day? Then bury somebody in the family every year thereafter for, like, 10 years, including one of your cousins who took a bullet to the head and you can see where they filled in the hole?

Me? I want a viking funeral. If you want to put a plaque down, go ahead, but you don't really need to waste the space.

Life is not about being careful, it's about sliding in and going: 'Holy shit, what a ride.' And that's it, it's okay to be overwhelmed.

Work with your therapist, work with your friends. I know it's hard to find the one, if you are divorced or if you're single or whatever it is, but eventually, everybody deserves their wow. Be patient with yourself and be patient with them. Seek first to understand and then to be understood.

If there's something going on with your significant other, whatever it is, talk it out. Try not to take it personally because a lot of the time it's past history and we all have it. Everybody has triggers.

And if it's new, it doesn't matter if you've been dating for six months or six years, there's going to be a trigger and you may not know it. And you know what? We're fallible. We fuck up. We're human beings, we're not infallible. We're fallible and that's just the way it is, so being overwhelmed is okay. Being overwhelmed is okay. Get help, don't shut down, don't close down. Yeah, I've been there, done that and got the t-shirt, got the scars. Get out there and get some help. Talk to whoever is going to help, whether it's clergy, therapy or asking to be committed.

It's okay to be overwhelmed, it happens to everybody and you can get through it.

7

The attempt

Let's talk about the events around 12/22/19 and 12/23/19.

I have found this difficult but I also have found this cathartic. It's challenging to discuss this, but as my good friend Nick Peet said, it's like therapy.

That day was a difficult day. I'd hit my low point, my kids had moved out about a month before that because somebody influenced them to basically pack up and leave and we all know who that was, who said I wasn't healthy because of something that I did. That was my ex.

The divorce was difficult, bloody messy to be honest. It should have cost $20,000 but it ended up costing me more than $100,000. Somebody who I knew for 30 years pretty much flipped the script on me and had been in a struggle for a long time with her illness. 15 years, to be exact.

You hit your breaking point, enough is enough and that's when I pulled the trigger and decided that we needed to part company after 23 years of marriage and 30 years together. Relationships end, people move on, people grow apart, that's what happens.

I was once told by my first therapist Dena Bubrick: 'You'll know when you're done, when you look in the mirror and you've made up your mind and you've done everything you can.'

That's the type of guy I am. I exhaust all my resources, I do the best I can, I push forward.

Nobody can say that I wasn't a good husband, nobody can say that I'm not a good father. You can't say that, sorry. Have I made mistakes? Yes. Everybody makes mistakes and I've made plenty of them and I'll make plenty more but if you move on, you move forward.

Communication is key.

The divorce should have cost me $20,000 when it was 50-50. I was literally scraping by towards the end of the divorce. I was barely able to put it all together. I was struggling and I wasn't in a comfortable environment at home.

Then something happened with the gas meter a week after. There's a hole in the gas meter and I still to this day don't know what happened. The Wi-Fi cameras were off when we were all out of the house. I find that very odd and ridiculous.

That was early on in the divorce. Then I had to live in the same house, under the same roof as somebody who was very angry at me because I walked away. I never cheated. It didn't mean that I didn't look, it didn't mean that I didn't have offers but I never cheated and I did the best that I could with what I had.

What should have cost me $20,000 ended up costing me probably over $100,000 so when I sold the house, my check went to my lawyer for the disbursement of the funds and it went to my credit guy. That's how desperate I was. I was broke, desperate, confused, sad, angry, all of it. All at once.

It was relieving to get the divorce, but I kind of knew the way it was going to go when we both agreed that we should meet this on a united front with the kids and then my ex looked at the kids the next morning — and the kids knew it was coming — and broke the news to them. She said: 'Your father asked me for a divorce and I agreed.'

I looked at her and I was like: 'Really? You just fucked up these kids. You just fucked up these kids.'

Put it on me. You know what, put it on me. I've taken the weight of shit since I was 12 years old so put it on me. I'm an underdog, I don't quit, I don't stop.

Unfortunately, I broke. The next day I looked for a spot to park the car and jump off the Tobin Bridge...

Not long ago, I took a knife, sat in my kitchen and tried to slit my throat. I made the cut, I had stitches. Why? Because I got some money from my mother — she left me some bonds — and I cashed them, but I didn't manage it correctly and that's my fault.

I'll take ownership of it. I didn't know the impact the divorce would have. I didn't know the impact it would have on me. To this day, I can't even drive through Norfolk anymore, and I still have a hard time because I have 19 years of memories in that house.

It was the third home my ex-wife and I bought. The neighborhood and everybody in it turned their back on me. They'd known me for 19 years. I'd helped them to move furniture, I'd watched their kids and everybody just turned their backs on me, just like that.

I hit the bottom and then what happened was I wasn't managing my money correctly, I was confused and scared. The first weekend when I was alone without my kids, when it was 50-50, I was like: 'What do I do?'

You have to learn to be alone again, as my good friend big dog John Johnson said to me. That's hard. Even though the marriage was going sideways, it was fucking hard.

I remember sitting in my apartment in Plainville and going: 'What do I do now, on a Sunday, by myself?' I borrowed some money from my mother's account that was used to pay for her nursing home. I borrowed $2500 because I was desperate. I didn't have any money; my credit cards were maxed out. I went to Jordan's Furniture — this was before I got my bonds — to get credit and they would only give me two or three grand. I needed four or five grand to get my furniture, so I borrowed it. I borrowed $2500. God forbid, even though I was the power of attorney for my mother, God rest her soul, the proxy and the executive of the state.

People in the family looked at me like I did something wrong.

My intention was to pay that $2500 back. Should I — and I'm going to judge myself — pay that back when I cash my 30 grand in bonds? Yeah. But I got wrapped up in my head and it was my mistake. I should have just paid it right back.

So, what happened was I got behind, took the kids on vacation, got further behind and then bang, I saw a big bill from the nursing home. I go: 'Fuuuuuuuuuuck.' It was like six or seven grand and I'm thinking 'What do I do?'

I panicked. I'm depressed. I just broke up with someone who I thought was the person after going through 30 other women. The dating process, at this age, sucks because people aren't who they say they are. People haven't owned their shit. People haven't got it together and they're not making progress.

I'm in progress, I'm not perfection. Am I perfect? No. But at least I try.

I'm not saying that I dated the women for a long time. They were one-offs and three-offs. You go out with them once and they blow you off or you go out with them three times and you think it's going somewhere and then you get ghosted. It's a shit show.

Unfortunately, most of the people that I run into have an addiction problem, whether that be smoking, drinking, or something they're covering up or they haven't got any real work done.

Fuck man, I've been in therapy for between 12 and 15 years. I've watched somebody go through alcoholism recovery and then go through a divorce. As my therapist Norman Gross says: 'It's a death of a marriage.' And I'm not saying my ex made it easy when I was in the house for six months, living with her.

This was a 50-50 divorce. Everything was across the board when we walked. Six months later, we're in the mediator room with the two lawyers because we're not going to court and my lawyer looks at me and says: 'What do you think?'

'You don't want to know what I think' was my response. The meeting should have lasted three hours but it went on for eight-and-a-half hours.

I looked at my wife and I said: 'See, see…'

So, this is my time to throw some shit. Am I actually? Why not, it's my fucking book. I'll do what I want.

She didn't make it easy, she made it miserable. I tried to do the best I could for her and my kids. So, somebody in my family reached out to my ex about the *Go Fund Me* page and said that I had put up the page. The phone call went through and my kids moved out. They still haven't told me why or what it meant to them and I live with that every day.

Have I stopped feeling guilty about it? Yeah. Because I've been thinking about something for the past three years and that's a very deep quote from Mark Twain: 'Forgiveness is the fragrance that is shared by the violet on the heel that has crushed it.' Think about that. I realized that the first person that I had to forgive was me.

I attempted suicide twice. I woke up in McLean Hospital on Christmas Eve. That's where I spent my Christmas week and I learned a ton. A year before, I was at Norwood and I didn't learn shit because something went wrong. There was a chemical imbalance, it was mental illness. They say remission. Fuck you, I'm cured. I decided to be cured. Nobody needs to monitor me.

The first time I was in Norwood, in lockdown, I couldn't align with anybody. I didn't get it. The second time I went to my therapist's office and he saw my scar and he heard my story about going to the Tobin Bridge and looking for a spot to park the car to jump off it, he committed me. I told him I wasn't going back to Norwood. I went to McLean and somebody violated the rules and contacted my ex, who's a nurse, to tell her where I was. I didn't even get a chance to explain to my kids that I had tried to commit suicide. I wasn't given that opportunity. Am I pissed about it? Fuck, yeah, I'm pissed. They're my kids too. Am I angry? You'd better believe I'm angry about a couple of things. Did I forgive myself? Yeah, it took me a long time and somebody we know kept throwing guilt at me.

'You should be paying more, you stole the money...' I stole the money? Fuck off. You haven't lived like me. Those members of the family who weren't nice about it, they know who the fuck they are. I'm not gonna call them out but they know who they are, stirring the pot and reaching out to my ex. Fuck right off.

You wonder why I don't talk to you? Fuck off, just fuck off. We're not connected anymore. Because your nana died, my mother who I'd known for 54 years and you're going to judge me? You can't walk a day in my shoes.

My father died when I was 12. I'd get the shit kicked out of me every fucking day. I built myself up, started my own company and I've had a ton of help. Thank God for friends.

I always remember one of my top clients, back in the early 2000s, God rest his soul, saying to me that you can pick your friends but you can't pick your family.

What is it about family that they think they can open their mouths and judge you just because they have the same last name? Especially in today's world. They need to get over their entitlement complex. You ain't entitled to shit. You call people sir, you call people uncles, you call people dad, you call people mom. My kids would never say Kevin.

That day was like any other day. I even thought about sticking my arm in the garbage disposal in the hope it would kill me. I had all these fucked up thoughts and they just would not go away. No matter what I did. Eating was hard, shitting was hard. Forget about getting a fucking erection, forget about that too. I was dating some-body and it was all just weird. The only reason I was dating her was to take up my time because that's all you want, you want somebody to take up your fucking time so that you don't have to think.

I couldn't do yoga, I couldn't do exercise, I couldn't do anything.

In the movies, one cut and it would all be over but that's not true. That didn't happen. I looked at myself as I was bleeding all over my hand and I'm holding the knife. As I was holding the knife, I'm like: 'What did you do? You've got daughters.'

I was out of my skull, it just didn't make any sense to me and then I was like: 'Okay, let's go to the hospital.'

I made up some story and they sewed me up and then I lied to the woman I was dating. I made something up about falling on the shovel or something because how do you have that conversation?

'Oh, by the way, I tried to commit suicide twice.' Yeah, it's not easy. Now, it's not a problem. It took me a while but when I'm dating now, it comes out in the second or third date because I'm going to throw it out there.

I'm 55 years old and when I'm dating somebody, I have to get it all out there. I don't want to wait six months and tell them that I had mental illness and that I tried to kill myself.

How do you have that conversation with yourself?

This particular person that I was dating six, seven, eight months ago said: 'Your first book went through your mother, maybe you shouldn't have said certain things.' Fuck off. It's my experience. Okay, my mom was not happy that I said in there that my father was an alcoholic. He was. It doesn't mean he was a bad guy. That's what it was like when I was 12 and the kids know.

They're not stupid, they'll figure it out. You can only protect them so much, they're not dumb.

I woke up on Christmas morning at McLean Hospital. I was like: 'Okay, I guess this is how I'm spending Christmas.' They had classes and stuff and I learned a lot and then I found out about ECT. I didn't even research it because you don't have your phone.

I wanted to try it. They told me about the process and the procedure and how many treatments I needed and I remember getting wheeled down to an ECT lab and I'm sitting there thinking: 'What am I doing?' As they put the needle in my arm, I almost told them to stop, I almost shit myself. I almost didn't have Yuki, heroic courage. And then something snapped into me. I think it was my Dad and he said: 'Do it, Kevin. You've got to do something. Medication's not working, training's not working, therapy's not working, nothing's working.'

I was in the blackest black hole I've ever been in in my life. I'd never been there before and it was the worst experience of my life next to my father dying, next to seeing my Dad in a coffin three or four times a day for a week. I didn't feel like me. I couldn't get right with myself, I didn't feel normal.

No wonder people drink and eat and all the rest of it. I didn't feel normal. I felt worthless and I felt stupid.

My kids left. I wasn't even a father. My business was failing, the whole nine yards. Thank God for all my clients who stayed with me. I was faking it the whole time. Faking it at client's houses, just faking it and then I would get in my car to drive home and go 'Fuck, man.'

I was on autopilot when I was training clients. Fucking autopilot. Thank God I didn't have a lecture or anything else to do. Who knows how that would have fucking come out. And then by the third ECT treatment, I'm like: 'Hey, man, I'm feeling normal. I'm feeling like Kevin Kearns. I'm feeling like Coach Kearns again. Wow, this works.' Then I became friends with the ECT people at McLean.

They're great, they're warriors. And then there was the IV ninja. She came in one day and put in an IV line that I didn't even know was there. She's talking to me one day, probably three, four, five months into it, and she says that they fight the stigma every day.

I sat there and thought: 'Fuck, you know what, I'm guilty. I'm guilty of the stigma of mental illness.' The whole time in my head, my ego took over: 'I'm a man, I can handle it.' I kept telling myself to suck it up. I didn't understand the concept of being over-whelmed. It's like being in a plane and everything falls apart.

Imagine that. Struggling. Fighting every day. Trying to manage moment to moment and not knowing a way out and not wanting to burden your friends.

Well, now I'm back but I'm not back really because I'm a new Kevin. As a good friend of mine, the old marketing guru Ron Weinberg said: 'You're different, Kev' and I was like: 'Yeah, man. Nobody's going to fucking stop me now.'

You don't like the fact that I'm brash, you don't like the fact that I'm real, that I'm outspoken? I'm fucking raw because that's what we need in this world: raw and real.

It's okay to get angry. Anger is useless unless you channel it but everybody gets angry. Was I angry at myself for doing what I did? Yeah. I've got kids, man. Of course, I was angry at myself. I had to let go of it. It was just a point in my life that happened, and I had to let go. Let's go and move on. I forgave myself. I became okay with me. I became the right person in the world. And thank God for friends like Craig Rose who drove me weekly to ECT therapy, the support of my therapists, and the support of my friends like Lionel Beane, Jamie Burke, Keith Foster, Steve Whittier.

It was the happiest day when I told Craig that I wouldn't be going back to ECT therapy. 'You put the work in for six months. I'm good and it's all thanks to you.'

For a while, I enjoyed it but it's in my back pocket. They said they're going to miss me and they're glad that I'm on my own path. 'You look good, you've done the work, you came out of it.'

Yeah, I came out of one of the most difficult diseases and illnesses there is. It's an insidious disease. It's like alcoholism. It's like addiction because your chemicals change in your brain and you can't figure it out. I could have complained about it and bitched about it. Kind of like what's going on in the world today but it was my choice to fix it.

Are you going to bitch about it or do something about it? I did something about it.

And if you're going through this, absorb whatever you fucking can when I tell you that it's going to be okay. It will be okay. Ask for help, go to your friends, go to your priest, your clergy, whatever it is, whoever you can talk to. Talk to somebody and the moment they judge you, fucking walk away.

Becoming transparent is the true essence of being a human being.

Whether you're in yoga, martial arts or fitness, you know who your true friends are. Don't hesitate, reach out. If they're real friends, they will grab your hand like I will. That's why I'm writing this book. I want to get this out to everybody. It's necessary. It's needed because we all have some type of PTSD and depression. Especially now with what's going on. We're locked in, we can't do this, we can't do that. You can't exercise because the gyms are closed but you can drink because the liquor stores are open. Are you fucking kidding me?

Reach out to people. Use the hotline. Money doesn't matter if you're dead so don't be so busy chasing the green.

Courage is not the absence of fear. Courage is having to do what you have to do in the face of fear.

If the state trooper didn't pull me over, I probably would have done it. That's why, when you're near bridges, you see signs for the Samaritans because people jump off bridges.

When you're depressed, when you're anxious, when you're scared, when you're frightened and you're in that black hole and you want to just end it, that's the worst fear of all and you have to step up. You have to reach your arm up and ask for help.

If you're feeling desperate and alone, you're not. Reach out to whoever you're going to reach out to and, most of all, forgive yourself. You have to dive into yourself, you have to accept the help and you have to go to the experts.

It's not your fault that you have mental illness but it's your job to find a way to fix it. You're going to have to own it, forgive yourself and move forward. Don't look back, hold your vision, keep your passion, maintain and invest in perseverance and remember that you're stronger than you think you are.

8

Guilt, regret and shame

When you look at things when you"re down a hole and you go down that path of trying to end your life, there's so much emotion that comes with that. It's a selfish act and it's also being in a place that you can't explain to anyone, you really can't.

It's been, like, 19 months and it's in the back of my head a lot. My younger daughter is back with me and she gave me a card that said: 'I'm sorry I wasn't there for you, Dad.' That's a lot to take in. By the same token, she said that she was glad that I was always there for her, except at one point I wasn't.

It's tough being sensitive. It makes you a good coach and a good parent but it's a lot to manage. I wear my heart on my sleeve. Fuck it. It is what it is. I've managed my guilt, I've managed my shame and my regret and it's a daily process. How do you get over that pouring sky?

You have to get out there after you get divorced. How do you have that fucking conversation? 'Oh, by the way, I tried to commit suicide twice. By the way, it was in a lockdown year. By the way, I had ECT therapy.' How do you throw that out there? How do you take the risk of throwing that out there and saying: 'Here's who I am…' Love me, hate me, whatever…'

As a martial artist, somebody who has been stood on, stomped on, stepped on and all that stuff, you have a code. You don't want to ever hurt anybody. You try not to ever hurt somebody's feelings but that's next to impossible. You know someone 30 years old and still do not know them.

Guilt, regret and shame. That's a hard one. I've dealt with that a lot. I'm still dealing with that. And when you fuck up, you're going to fuck up because everything is going on at once. It's not an excuse, it's just fact. We're humans, we're fallible, I'm fallible. The problem is that sometimes I think I'm not.

It's hard to be the granite in the family, to be the driving force, to be rock solid and never fall apart. I always remember a scene from the movie *Fury* with Brad Pitt, where he's this rough and tumble sergeant. One of his gunners is dead with his brain half-blown out in the seat. They then get a new gunner. He's going back to base, to get his orders, and he tells the guys he's going to have a smoke. He goes behind the building and just falls apart and has his moment.

Sometimes you feel so much for somebody that you want them to have the confidence you have to have that empowerment and then sometimes you push it too hard. Sometimes you forget that they're not ready and that they want you to back off.

Maybe I'm not ready. Lots of things take time. Guilt, regret, shame, it takes a lot, especially if you've been raised Catholic and that's not a dig, it's just a fact.

A client of mine, who was a Catholic — back when my ex and I were going through IVF — said that the reason we couldn't have children was because we didn't go to church often enough.

'What did you say to me?'

It's never easy experiencing guilt, shame and regret. Forgiving yourself is the first thing, then apologizing with a real apology, meaning it and then trying to move on. Moving on is the tough part because I may appear rough and tumble but I beat myself up constantly. 'What if I'd done this better? What if I'd done that better?'

Maybe in my past of being bullied, maybe it was my fault. Maybe they'd have left me alone if I hadn't have said this or that.

Why me? That's the other question that sits in my mind. You lose your father at 12 and you say: 'Why me?'

Your marriage goes sour after 23 years and you say: 'Why me?'.

Your kids move out because you have some mental health challenges and you say: 'Why me?'

You hurt a loved one, you ask the same question, you ask yourself why you did it and at the end of the day, it sucks. 'Why the fuck did I do that?' Maybe you weren't thinking. You might have been caught up in the moment, caught up in whatever was going on. Who knows?

Guilt and regret will kill many men. It's hard and I don't like it but it is what it is. Shame, on the other hand, that stuff... Am I ashamed that I tried to commit suicide twice, one day after the other? Yeah, I'm fucking ashamed of it.

I'm supposed to be Coach Kearns, I'm supposed to be an MMA guru, blah, blah, blah...

At the end of the day, I keep forgetting that I'm just a man trying to do the best I can and that's all anybody can do. Then you go out and try to find someone in your 50s, who has the same values as you that has honest appreciation, honest affection, honest communication and loyalty. That's not easy.

It's a learning process. You've got your stuff, they've got their stuff, you've got your baggage, they've got their baggage and you try to make it work and you fuck up. It happens, it sucks. It hurts them, it hurts you. Then you play it over in your mind, wondering what you could have done differently, what you could have said differently... This happened, that happened...

My goal was never to make anybody feel uncomfortable unless they're trying to make somebody else feel uncomfortable. That's when I stepped in. I'm always trying to make people feel comfortable, make them feel at ease, at peace and then I have my own internal war going on at the same time.

I always say to people: 'Shoulda, woulda, coulda...' Then I don't practice what I preach. I'm always like 'I shoulda done this, I coulda done that, why did I do that?' Sometimes the why, who knows? We're complicated, we're not monkeys. Monkeys eat, shit and have sex. We're more complicated than that.

Guilt, regret, shame, they're all hard. And then there's trying to have the ability to let go and do your thing, do your best to make amends to them and to yourself.

I can look at it and say that I made mistakes with my kids. I made mistakes with other people that are important in my life but what do you do? It's only a mistake if it's not a lesson learned, so you try to learn the lesson. You try to be more in touch, in tune, in the moment and not let the moment get away from you. You hope there's a next time, you prepare yourself as best as you can.

Sometimes with me, my need to make people feel better, to gain more confidence, it gets the best of me. That need to empower people sometimes makes me rush the process myself. Life is a process but it needs to help give people in my life the edge, that empowerment, the confidence to be able to handle situations, that's my own ego. Maybe not even ego, maybe it's more that I have a need to be the superhero, a need to be Batman, the need to be protective but Batman can't be everywhere…

Shit goes sideways all the time and then you worry whether everything is covered. You can't not be a martial artist or an entrepreneur and not be a little worried all the time. That's what you do. There's a lot of worrying, especially with loved ones and with mental health.

At the end of the day, do the best you can. Give maximum effort, every day. You've done it or you've fixed it, the best you can. You have to fix it for them and fix it for yourself and then hopefully you mediate the guilt, the regret and the shame, none of which is particularly easy.

It's pretty emotional. I'm a pretty emotional guy. What can I say? I want this to be raw and real. I hope this helps somebody. I hope it helps somebody moving forward.

Make it a great day.

9

The power of forgiveness

There's a great quote from Mark Twain and that is: 'Forgiveness is the fragrance that is shared by the violet on the heel that has crushed it.'

JUST THINK ABOUT THAT.

THE FIRST PERSON you have to forgive is yourself.

TO TRANSLATE THAT QUOTE, somebody spits in my face but I've got to forgive them. That's not easy because you want to retaliate — an eye for an eye. You want to rip their throat out, I get it. I've been there, done that and still want to do that sometimes.

BUT WHAT I realize after going through at least two years of my own mental illness — of which I'm cured because I choose to be — is that the power of forgiveness is interesting.

. . .

IT SHOULDN'T BE CALLED hindsight, it should be called Kindsight because how do you know until you've gone through with it?

IT'S like dealing with a kid. You tell them not to touch the stove because they're going to burn themselves. Eventually, they touch the stove and burn themselves.

'DON'T PLAY with the scissors, you're going to cut yourself.' 'Experience is a great teacher.

You can't put a timeframe on learning, you can't put a timeframe on love, you can't put a timeframe on anything. Sometimes, it happens in a flash and sometimes it takes time.

THIS — they call it your gut — knows. This is intelligent, this is intuitive, this knows. It's not in your head

— that's monkey mind. It's not what happens to you, it's your interpretation of what happens to you.

I LOVE the fact that I run my own business, that I have to answer text messages, emails, that I have to respond to Facebook, Instagram, LinkedIn but at the same time, it's challenging, so you have to remember to forgive yourself first.

IT'S okay to be a little self-centered, to take a little self-care. To take care of you.

. . .

ONE OF THE best ways to look at it is, if you can't help you, you can't help others and if you can't forgive you, then you can't move forward.

I DIDN'T GET a chance to tell my kids that I tried to commit suicide. My ex did that for me and that's another thing entirely. I was overwhelmed. I crashed, I burned and became the phoenix I am now. I'm the phoenix rising. You really have to sit down and forgive yourself because if you can forgive yourself, you can forgive other people. It doesn't mean you forget. Forgiveness is not forgetting. Forgiveness is clearing the path so that you can take care of your side of the street.

IT'S the same as with my ex-brother-in-law. He was married to my sister and I reached out to him about a year ago. He was trying to be my friend. I said: 'No, that's not what I want. I'm just saying we're cool. I don't want to hear from you, I don't want to know what you're doing, your business, what went on with my sister. I don't care. All I'm saying is that we're clean. Done. Don't reach out to me again. I forgive you for the past but I'm not going to forget.'

THAT'S the way it works. I forgive you but I'm not going to forget. You will not gain my trust again.

WHAT YOU CAN REALLY GIVE your friends, your loved ones, is your time, your attention, your appreciation, your trust and your love. Your patience as well. That's it. That has a huge return on investment and when somebody violates that trust, they get pushed out.

I have this saying: 'Lago, medio and quarto.' That means long, medium and close range. I start people outside of the circle, then gradually bring them closer until they're at close range. Once they're there, I'll lay down in traffic for them but if you violate that, I'll keep pushing you out to the point where you might be pushed out past the long range.

THAT MEANS you're out of the circle and that's the way it is.

WHEN YOU'RE YOUNGER, you can fall too fast and trust somebody too quickly. Once they hook you in, they can flick a switch and think: 'Now I've got you, I don't have to maintain anything.'

BULLSHIT.

YOU HAVE TO FORGIVE YOURSELF.

THERE WAS A DOCTOR — I forget her name — 20 or 30 years ago and she talked about relationships. She had two potted plants with big leaves. She had one that was wilted and brown and the next one which was green. She goes: 'Most people think their relationships and their marriages look like a healthy plant, but in reality, they look like an unhealthy plant.'

SHE TOOK OUT GREEN PAINT, painted the unhealthy leaves and said that's what people do in their relationships and marriages. 'They think that's enough.'

THERE'S A SAYING that the grass is always greener on the other side but I counter that with the grass being greener wherever you water it, spend time and attention on it and fertilize it.

. . .

FORGIVE YOURSELF, appreciate yourself, don't be so hard on yourself and if you think you can do better, you go do better.

I'M ALWAYS LEARNING, whether that be relationships — business or romantic — whether that be myself, yoga, whatever it is.

FORGIVE YOURSELF, always keep learning and raise your standards.

WE OVERANALYZE the past but we can't fix it. If you run to what's in front of you, you will escape what's behind you.

WE ALL HAVE GIFTS, don't keep them wrapped. Do you think I want to be here, talking about some of the darkest times in my life? No. Is it cathartic? Yes. Could it help some people? Yes. Well, that's why I'm doing it.

FORGIVE yourself and then you can forgive other people. Appreciate you, think about what got you to where you are. Think about what you've gone through to get to where you are now, to get to that place.

MAYBE EVERYTHING you went through was to get you to where you are now, to get you to that person, to that job, to that career, whatever it is.

. . .

FORGIVE YOURSELF FIRST. It's okay to be a little self-centered because to be self-centered is to take care of yourself.

YOU'VE GOT to have honest communication with yourself and honest communication with your significant others but to do that you have to forgive yourself first.

10

The way back

Let's talk about the way back... It's been a long haul. It's taken me since last January and feeling better from the ECT that I've turned my life around. It's been a long journey and it's been an interesting journey. I was told that instead of putting a good or bad label on it, it's just an experience.

It's something I had to go through to get to where I am now.

After 23 years of marriage and 30 years with the same person, you can look back and say that you could have done things differently and at the end of the day, it's devastating, it's a failure, it's the death of a relationship but shit happens. When you mediate that — and I've been through a lot of this with clients that have gone through this — you don't realize how tough it is until you go through it.

The way back has been very interesting though. I'm sitting in a loft apartment in Cumberland, overlooking the Blackstone River every morning with 17-foot ceilings and one of my daughters is in the other room.

Back in 1929 or 1930 before the big telescope went up, they thought there was one galaxy with 100 million stars in it. When they put the new one up, they realized there's 100 million stars in it with

100 million galaxies and it's expanding. I don't know how it works but it is what it is.

I've always tried to remember that: everything happens for a reason. We might not like the reasons but it's the way you put it together.

I am relentless. You've got to be relentless. You've got to be relentless in feeling better. You've got to drive forward. You can't look back and you've just got to keep going.

And then you take a page from the top of my book. You don't want to think about the light at the end of the tunnel, you want relief now.

When you blend in with the surroundings, you can tell when something is too black because it doesn't make sense. There's always some light in nature, even when it's dark and when it's too black, something's wrong.

ECT worked for me. The carnivore diet works for some, while others use CBD and THC. ECT fixed me within a week and the specialists were dumbfounded.

Pay attention to your nutrition, obviously. Pay attention to alcohol not being a good substitute because it's a depressant. Some people get really, really down on it versus getting really, really up. Luckily, I got up from it. I'm the fun drunk, for lack of a better description.

If you have to use medication for a while, that's okay. Use it and then eventually, hopefully, you'll get off the medication. There are other ways, though, and you should explore them. Most of the time, people will push to increase the level of medication. Maybe you need it, maybe you don't.

One of the best releases I get is from training. When I got really depressed, even training wasn't fun. It wasn't fun to me anymore and it's always been my go-to. Whenever I've been angry or sad or upset, I go right to that, I go right to training, whether that be yoga, hitting pads, hitting sticks, or strength and conditioning, whatever it is. If you're trying to come out of it and I came out of it, that's where I would go. This is how I spin it: it's almost like flying. I remember the first time I flew to Alaska in 2010 to do two seminars and made four thousand dollars for the two days.

I asked the guy who hit me up and got me to come out: 'How long's the flight?' He was like: '10 hours.'

I was like: 'Eurgh'. And then when I saw the guy again at a different conference and he wanted me to fly out, I said to myself: 'What, am I stupid? I'm gonna get four thousand dollars for four days to go to a place that I may never go otherwise, that may not be on my bucket list.'

The whole time on the plane, I just kept telling myself that time moves forward and that the plane is gonna get there some time.

It's the same thing with your recovery — or the big bounce, as I call it — every fall from grace brings you to the next level.

That's the whole point. When you're down, the real growth happens. I didn't realize that, to be honest. In the midst of all the shit that I had going on, I didn't realize that at all. It was very gratifying that my youngest moved back in with me about a month ago and she said: 'Dad, you did the best thing for me.'

'I know it was probably really hard for you and really difficult for you to give me space and to just let me figure it out on my own.'

I replied: 'Yeah. It was just as bad, if not worse, than when my father died.'

Dealing with that, not having them around for 18 or 19 months, was really difficult and that's what pushed me over the edge, when they moved out. Anybody who knows me knows who had a hand in that but it is what it is.

When I came back from that my business was just starting to pick up and then boom, COVID hit. Real growth, it comes when you get knocked down. I was in a bad relationship. It wasn't good. It was toxic and it went sideways. The reason you get into something like a toxic relationship is that you just want somebody to take up your time and space.

It wasn't a good decision, it was a bad decision. I just wanted something to take up my time because you can't watch the time when you're that depressed. You can't watch the time because it feels like the day is never going to end.

Stay patient with yourself and when it comes to the big bounce, be patient with yourself. Exercise. You've got to find something you like. Don't exercise and do something you freaking can't stand, that's stupid. If you hate running, why are you gonna take up running? If you hate spinning, why are you gonna take up spinning? Do what you love. I don't care if you're walking, I don't care if you're swimming, I don't care if it's holding pigeon pose for an hour at yoga. You just have to do whatever makes you feel better or feel complete or what brings you that sense of joy. Other people shouldn't even exist in the room, you should just do your own thing.

Sometimes I train with other people and yeah, I love it but at other times I want to train on my own with my sunglasses on my hat. That's basically me saying: 'Fuck off. It's just about leaving me to do my own thing.'

When I'm with a training partner, sometimes I lose my patience when I really just want to flow. The biggest word is patience and you've got to have perseverance. And find what you love. It doesn't matter how long it takes, time is irrelevant.

Abraham Lincoln was a failure until he was, like, 44 years old and he didn't live that long back then. He's on money, for crying out loud. There's a huge statue of him and he was a failing attorney.

How do you want to go down at the end of the day? How do you want people to remember you? I want to be left with a legacy. He tried and I'm trying. I try my best every fucking day. I get up and I try my best, whatever it is.

This morning, I had to go out real quick for something and my daughter had an asthma attack. I went out and bought her an inhaler because her other one was out and then I stopped by the store to get two gallons of water. This was at, 4:30-5am, and not one person says good

morning to the woman behind the counter. It's a beautiful day, the sun's coming out, it's 55 degrees. Do you think she wants to be there? Probably not.

As everybody knows, I'm a name badge guy, so I put up the gallons of water and I'm like: 'Oh, hey, Kim.'

She's like: 'How do you know my name?' I told her it was on her name badge and she said: 'Oh, thanks, I appreciate that.'

The sweetest words in any language are a person's name.

I try to make people's day whenever I can. I try to do what I can, when I can, not only for myself but for other people. There should be no payout, you should just do it. There should be no expectation of reciprocation.

As Corey Wayne says with Dr Wayne Dyer, an act of kindness not only raises the serotonin levels of the receiver, it raises the serotonin levels of the person giving and the people witnessing it.

It's taken me almost a year to finish this book and I could beat myself up about it but maybe I wasn't ready to finish it. My first book should have been launched in 2011 and then it came out in 2013 because the first ghostwriter ripped me off and took $4000 that a client gave me. I got disenfranchised with the whole thing and then one thing led to another before I found Kit Birmingham, my new ghostwriter. She jumped on board and the first thing she asked me is what I want to do with the book. I said that I wanted to help some people. If I get one person to read the book and turn their life around, I've done my job because everybody can equate and relate to always being picked last.

I grew up with superhero friends and I try my best to be a superhero every day. If you're going through hell, good, just keep going. Put one foot in front of the other. And I get it, man, believe me, I know how hard it is. I know how tough it is. I know how much you don't want to get out of bed in the morning, how much you don't want to go to work or do this or do that and you've got to push yourself.

People in a marriage, when their sex life goes sideways, they have to push themselves to have that intimacy. One of Dr Oz's suggestions is, if the kids are gone, go to bed naked because there are no barriers and it's a lot easier to have sex. And it's the same thing, you have to push yourself. People get complacent but complacency is death. You can't get complacent, you just can't. If I don't make the special person in my life fall in love with me every day, I'm not doing my job. Don't get stuck in a rut.

My foundations are real simple: honest communication, honest appreciation.

Don't get stuck in the wake of your life. You are important, you can do it. If I can do it, you can do it. Other people have done it.

It has not been an easy road. If you read my first book, you'll know. Low-income neighborhood, father dies at 12 and I did it. You can't be the victim. It's either victim or victor and I don't mean victory over other people, I mean victory over yourself, over your thoughts and feelings.

Feelings are just information but once it's in your brain you have judgment over it. 'Why am I feeling sad? I shouldn't be feeling sad.' Maybe you're just feeling sad. It's the same with anger. Maybe it's just a trigger. Constructively look at it. It's okay, forgive yourself. You're human, you're fallible, the only perfection is nature.

The sun rises, the sun sets, the grass grows, the rain falls. Only nature is perfect.

Be relentless and always make it a great day. May light, love and peace shine on you every day.

11

How I came back

Let's talk about ECT. Electroconvulsive therapy. Basically, they put you under and they zap you. They induce a public seizure and they reset the hard drive in your brain.

Unfortunately, for most of us that have gone through it, it was demonized in Hollywood. It's been out since 1938. It has a 90-95 per cent success rate in curing clinical depression, PTSD and bipolar, you name it.

For all you Hollywood people out there who decided to demonize it, go fuck yourselves.

I had a well-meaning doctor client, I won't say who it was, who wasn't a psychologist that told me that I shouldn't have done it. I'm like: 'It fixed me.'

I tried therapy, I tried drugs and nothing was working. It usually takes 12 treatments but after three treatments I was feeling better. I think I'm one of the best test cases.

I remember finding out about it at McLean when I spent a week there around Christmas time. I tried to take my life in 12/22/19 with a steak knife, and realized: 'What the fuck did I do?' and then the next day, I tried to jump off the Tobin Bridge.

My therapist then committed me and I said that there was no way that I was going to Norwood, which I did a year ago and it just didn't work. I played the game and got out because I was with homeless people.

My therapist committed me, I woke up on Christmas Eve in McLean Hospital and was there for a week.

It was a very strange beginning and then a couple of days into it I heard about the ECT stuff and it appealed to me so I decided to grab it. I didn't know much about it. I hadn't done any research into it. I didn't have a computer, I didn't have a phone, they took everything away. The people were nice and I figured that I should give it a shot because nothing else worked. Therapy wasn't working, exercise wasn't working, it takes hold of your life. It's miserable, it's awful, it sucks and you just feel like it's a bottomless pit, hence why I named the book *There's Light In The Tunnel*.

The old cliché is that there is light at the end of the tunnel. When you're in the middle of this shit

— and it is shit — you feel like you have no way out, you feel like you're worthless, you feel like you suck, you feel like everything you touch turns to shit. You don't realize that blowing up a 30- year relationship — even though it's necessary, which it was, and it feels good to a certain degree

— changes your life completely. It fucks with your mind, fucks with your brain, it fucks with everything, your whole sense of being. Going from a married couple to a not married couple... It was awful. I'm not going to lie. I'm not going to pull punches — the first 10 years were great and the last 15 or so were a complete shit storm.

Her alcoholism kicked off in about 2005. One kid was two-and-a-half, the other was six months old and I didn't know what to do. All she did was eat, drink and smoke. The line in my head — from when my parents grew up — was: 'In sickness and in health'. It'll get better. It'll get better. It'll get better. It didn't get better and as Rolf Gates told me once: 'If you're starving, you'll eat garbage'. If you're starving for attention, starving for affection, you'll eat garbage. I was starving so I ate garbage.

Then there's the other things that kick in: the house, the money, the kids, not breaking up the family. At the end of the day, that's bad, because what are you teaching your kids? Are you teaching them that this is how relationships work? Relationships, marriage, they're complicated. They're not easy. And by the same token — it's beautiful. It's a dichotomy. It's black and white, it's north and south. There are going to be moments of absolute bliss and there is going to be moments of: 'Holy crap, how do we get through thare storm?'

That's just life and the old adage of: 'What doesn't kill you makes you stronger' is true. I think every fall from grace brings you higher. I think the hardest thing to do when you're facing challenges with loved ones is to take a step back and not take it personally.

At this point, I'm lucky enough now that I have somebody. I'm with somebody who I think is the one. She gets me, I get her, she is my wow. Sometimes it takes 50-plus years to find out what you've always wanted, and I think that's where the concept comes in that: 'I don't love you because I need you, I need you because I love you.'

'I don't love you because I need you, I need you because I love you.' I need to have you in my life.

ECT was about talking about this to people and when you're out here, in the dating world, at 40, it's literally a shit show.

How do you bring this up in conversation? 'Oh, by the way, I was really sick and I tried to kill myself...' Yeah, that's an interesting conversation to have over a couple of drinks and a steak. Very difficult. It makes you very vulnerable. I would let it fly when I thought it was going to go some place — on the second or third date. What are you going to do? Wait four or five months, fall in love and then have the other person go: 'Woah, wait, slow it down...' I can't do that. I just can't do that. You've gotta pull the trigger. Swing for the fence, fuck it. Strength is vulnerability, vulnerability is strength. Courage is the absence of fear, courage is having to do what you have to do in the face of fear. And for those who I love, I will do both great things and terrible things, when necessary, and they know who they are and they know what that means.

I've always been one who has faced big challenges and one of my biggest challenges is to watch them go through pain. Having kids is a tough one, watching them go through pain. Watching your partner go through hard times is tough. I'd much rather take the shots myself. I'll take the bullets. I'd rather be full of bullet holes so that they don't have to go through it and so that I don't have to watch.

It's tough to sit back and watch somebody that you are truly, honestly that in love with suffer. Having them suffer or be in pain, it's just, it's tough and that's why the ECT thing helped. I've got to thank people like Craig Rose who drove me to my ECT therapy and the people there. I thank the beautiful people at McLean for everything they did for me. They know who they are. They knew what I was going through and they always checked in with me.

They always asked me how I was feeling and my response was always: 'I feel almost 100 per cent.' 'Why don't you feel 100 per cent?' they'd ask.

'Because I don't have my kids back.'

My kids moved out because my ex and somebody in the family were manipulative and used my situation and my mental illness against me.

I know me and I've been in a lot of stressful situations. One of which was my mother passing away from COVID on 12/24/20. She passed on her birthday and I sat with her for 11 hours, pulled the plug and watched her die.

After that, it all went sideways with the family. Not everybody. Just a few people had to be put in their place. Not to mention my ex not making it fun afterwards. She broke my balls because I didn't send the $250 for her child support on Christmas Day. Whoops, I forgot. Maybe I was a little preoccupied.

She then reminded me of two or three other bills that were due. She's making $150,000 a year and you're going to break my balls about a couple of hundred bucks? Really?

Not nice. Not nice at all. She's self-centered and everything is about her. Sadly, that's just the way it is and that's fine. You live and learn.

You can go back and beat yourself up and say: 'Why did I meet this person' but it is what it is. As far as you know, the struggle is the time to realize you're stepping up your game because it teaches you to go forward.

You step up, you put up, you go forward and that's what it is. You just keep running, you just don't stop, you just can't.

I tried the medication and they were saying that ECT was 12 treatments. Last August, it's been a year now, I spoke to Chris, the nurse practitioner who interviews you at the end and I asked him: 'Hey, how do I know when I don't need this anymore?'

He looked at me and he said: 'When you ask that question, Kevin.'

I looked him in the eye, told him I was good and he replied with: 'We're here when you need us.'

As my therapist Norman Gross would say: 'It's in your back pocket.' If you need a little reset, it's in your back pocket.

There are other therapies out there. There's Lightbox therapy, there's magnetics, a bunch of other stuff and you've got to try and see what works. If medication's working for you, great. Do I advocate for it? No. I know people are now using THC for anxiety and depression and it works.

People say it's a gateway drug. So's alcohol, so's nicotine, so's sugar. Over in Europe, they have a sugar tax, the amount of sugar in a Coke over there is 25 per cent compared to over here.

Addiction is addiction. It's always out there and it's always out there with the American attitude of 'More, more, more, more, more.' That's the problem.

Do I consider myself an addict? Nah.

The only thing you can change is the attitude within your thoughts. Pain is inevitable, suffering is a choice and that's from my friend Lee Jordan. Pain is inevitable, suffering is a choice and believe me, this is why they call it mental illness. It's an illness. It's not your fault, you didn't do anything wrong, it just happens. It becomes overwhelming. Whatever it is — changes of chemistry in your brain — it just fucks you up, whatever it is. Divorce, death, anything like that can trigger it and then it blows up in your face.

I do therapy. I'm still in therapy and I think everybody should be in therapy on a regular basis, to be honest. I think it's important to have therapy because you just can't do it on your own. You need an objective person to bounce stuff off, not subjective. Most family, unless they're close friends, will tell you flat out not to do it.

That's my piece on ECT and I hope you find it interesting.

12

From the crash to the climb back

This is my climb back up from getting crushed from a divorce — financially, emotionally, spiritually — the whole nine yards. From attempting suicide twice — on December 22, 2019 and then December 23, 2019.

THANK GOD MY THERAPIST, Norman, took me to hospital. It is just the maddest thing to ever happen to me.

THE GOOD NEWS is that I had electroconvulsive therapy. Hollywood can go fuck themselves because they demonized it in the 70s when they showed *One Flew Over The Cuckoos Nest* and I believe it was Danny DeVito getting ECT without an aesthesia. So Hollywood, fuck you, that shit works.

THEY RECOMMENDED 12 treatments before you start feeling better and I started feeling better after three so I'm a living example of the benefits of electroconvulsive therapy.

. . .

WHAT IS THAT? They basically induce a seizure in your brain to change its chemical balance. Shit works, it worked for me, it's been out since 1938 and it has between a 90 to 95 per cent success rate for curing PTSD, anxiety, depression and all that stuff. So, I'm going to go with that.

I LEARNED A LOT THAT WEEK. I woke up on Christmas Eve morning at McLean Hospital, which literally saved my life, because nothing else was working for six months to a year. You name it, meds weren't working, therapy wasn't working, it was all spiraling. Exercise wasn't working and that was my go-to for when I felt shitty and angry.

I HAVE FELT sadness before but this was different. This was something that was just uncontrollable.

I WENT in to be put back together — thank God. As I was getting wheeled down my first time, there was a little voice inside of me which said that I had to do it.

13

If you're starving, you'll eat garbage

If you're starving, you'll eat garbage

You're in a toxic relationship, a toxic marriage and you've been in it for many years and you have the kids, you have the house, the equity line, the IRA and all the rest of it and you're sitting there thinking about that marriage vow: 'In sickness and in health.'

If somebody has an addiction problem, you hang in there because yes, it's an illness, and yes, it's a choice to quit. It's also a family disease, as I know all too well because my father passed away from alcoholism when I was 12.

My mother got pissed, God rest her soul, when she read my first book because she believed my Dad wasn't an alcoholic. That was clear to me when I was 12. Kids know. They're not stupid, they'll figure it out. You can only protect them so much, they're not dumb.

So, if you're starving, you'll eat garbage and what that means is you fall in love, you get married and people do change over time. People change, people evolve and you either grow together or grow apart and you can't beat yourself up for that.

I'm really good at that, beating myself up, which probably led to where I went to and at the end of the day, when all the resources have been exhausted, you have to decide to pack it in.

You know, going through divorce sucks, even amicable ones. I have a friend of mine, Micah, who says he went through one completely amicably and he still needed therapy.

He goes: 'I can't imagine when it's messy.'

It's funny. People that you've known 20 to 30 years, people that you've been with and been intimate with, they just flip the script and I believe that shows a lack of personal responsibility.

So, if you're starving, you'll eat garbage. Take two-year-olds for example, when they're in the terrible twos and they're going through their shit. It's not that they're looking for positive or negative attention, it's just that they're looking for attention and it's almost the same thing. If you're starving, you'll eat garbage.

Attention and affection. You'll eat it because it's all you know. It's difficult, it sucks and it's not fun and then you get out into the real world and then you're completely jaded when you have to start over. You're fearful, you're scared, frightened beyond belief, you don't want to fall in love again and you're afraid of failing.

You're afraid of failing because when you look at divorce, it's the failure of a marriage and the failure of a relationship. It's a complete breakdown in communication and that's where the regret comes in, that's where the resentment comes in.

The good news is, if you're lucky enough to get out there and meet someone as you pass 40 and 50 or after your first divorce that you connect with, you can put your shit aside and not carry that cement overcoat as far.

Be there to support them as much as possible and vice versa. They have their shit, you have your shit and that's the way it is.

Getting out there in the dating world after age 40 is hard. I went through a lot of people. I didn't have sex with them, but they were one-offs or three-offs — and some you click with, some you don't. Sometimes you find out they have something underlying they're self-medicating with. They're drinking or they're workaholics. They're eating or they're exercising to extremes. They're gambling or they're sex addicts. You name it, it just goes on and on and on because they're self-medicating.

You could sit there and say that I compensated too. I tried to end my life. It's amazing when you forget what feeling loved is all about. You forget what unconditional love is.

There's a quote from Rumi: 'Even after all this time, the sun never says to the Earth: 'You owe me.' Look what happens with a love like that, it lights up the whole sky.'

When you're in an adult relationship, you have an opportunity to give. You're giving and not receiving. You're giving because you want to make the other person feel good, because you want to fulfill their needs, whatever those needs are. Whether it's putting the coffee maker on, stopping the car or doing the laundry, you're not doing it for the payback. If there's an expectation of reciprocation then it's not unconditional.

You do stuff for your kids, that's unconditional. You give your kids birthdays and Christmas presents and have no expectations so shouldn't it be the same for a romantic relationship, for your spouse, for your significant other?

The other thing I think you need to do when you connect with that person is give maximum effort.

You need to make them fall in love with you every day. You can't get complacent. If you do then what happens is you disconnect, you just go in opposite directions.

I think the toughest thing as a man to do is to shut up, listen and to not try and fix things. Women just want to be heard. Men just want to be heard too.

Seek first to understand and then to be understood.

We all want to be understood and then we all want to feel like we're right which I think is a waste of time. You want to tell the truth, to be effective.

We all want to feel right, we all want to have justice and sometimes when you're starving and you eat garbage, there is no justice.

When you've been stepped on, tortured, crushed and had your spirit ripped out, you've had it killed. People have done it for me. People have gone through messy divorces and the other person that they thought they knew better than any other, they killed their spirit, they crushed it and now they have to rebuild themselves. They have insecurities, they have underlying factors and it's awful.

Been there, done that, got the t-shirt and the wounds and the scars to prove it. When you get back out there, you all have wounds. You can't help it.

Picture your heart and soul like a pincushion and the person just keeps jabbing it. I always remember my mother's pincushion. It had all these needles in it and that's what your heart feels like. It feels like a punching bag. And no offense to the women out there, it's a hell of a lot harder for men because we have no recourse.

A friend of mine was a victim of domestic violence — scars, scratches, punches, the whole nine yards — and he wouldn't lift his hand. He's ex-military, ex-martial arts and he wouldn't lift the hand.

After the divorce was final, she said: 'I just did it to get you to do something.'

I felt that. I felt like my ex was in my face every day for seven months, in front of the kids. I stayed out of the house as much as possible. I can't remember from the time I pulled the trigger in September to the time when we sat down at the first meeting to go through the documents and she moved out. I don't remember anything of that seven months of my life. I remember some of the women I dated, I remember some of the fun that I had here and there but the rest of it, I don't remember. That's because if you're starving, you'll eat garbage.

People used to say that relationships are 50-50. No. When it's going well, it's 50-50 and those moments matter. But other times, it's 70-30 and sometimes 95-5 and that's when you get the real test of a relationship, the real test of a marriage, the real test of a friendship.

If you're a man in a room full of women, you have to bounce between being their friend and their romantic lover as well as their confidante because they can change like the weather.

My ex and I went through a lot of tough stuff and then I went sideways for 12 or 13 years. What did I do? I ate garbage because I was starving. I kept my mouth shut. I didn't say enough.

We didn't figure it out but I can't look back and fault that and say that I stayed in it too long. A lot of people ask me or make that statement that I stayed in it too long, they ask me if I wish for a different outcome. You can't wish, it is what it is. Maybe the reason you went through that was to get to where you're at.

I don't know what people who go through domestic violence go through. I don't know what that feels like. But I do know what it's like to be verbally, spiritually and emotionally abused, emasculated, belittled and bullied. Treated like dirt, treated like trash, not there enough, not enough of this, not enough that…

Occasionally, I'd get that I was a good father, a good provider and good at reinventing myself but words cut, they hurt. Why else do people say they're sorry? Why else do people say: 'I love you?' If words didn't matter, why do we have them?

I try to pick my words carefully. Sometimes I'm good at it, sometimes I'm not and the big thing is that we're all in progress. We're not infallible and that's tough to be okay with.

It's hard to sit there with your heart in your hand and ask for forgiveness when you fuck up. It's hard but it needs to be done. That's why millennials are saying: 'My bad.'

'My bad?' Fuck you, that's a pussy way. Yeah, I'm going to say it, you're a pussy.

All these idiots on social media that spout off, keep your mouth shut. Just keep your mouth shut. If you don't have anything good to say, don't say anything at all. If you can't say it on the playground, don't say it.

34 years in the business and I'm not gonna quit. I have one power: I never give up. And I won't.

I give 150 per cent to whatever I do, whether that be business, relationships, kids, romantic relationships, 150 per cent because I don't know anything else. I don't know quit and you shouldn't know quit either.

I'm going to use the word "should". Get that in your bones. Don't quit if you're going through hell, keep going.

If you're starving and you're eating garbage, maybe flip the script. Realize that, hit pause and then write down the things that work and the things that don't work. It's real simple.

It's real simple: honest communication, honest affection, honest appreciation and loyalty. There, done, it's easy. And don't get complacent. No matter whether you've been together 20 or 30 years, when you look at time, time is irrelevant. I've known people that dated for seven years, got married and it ended and I've known people who met with love at first sight, married three months later and have been married for 30 years. There is no formula. Trust your heart or your gut. Whatever you want to call it, just trust it.

Write your own script, write the story. You are the author of your story. So, if it's toxic, get out. Recognize the signs.

Everybody's got a little PTSD after going through a messy divorce and everybody's gun shy. No risk, no reward. That's how it happens. I'll fall down, flat on my face. Fuck it. I've failed plenty of times before, in business and in life. Fuck it. Get back up and dust yourself off. Life isn't all sunshine and rainbows. It's a very mean and nasty place and I don't care how tough you are, it will beat you to your knees and keep you there permanently if you let it. Nobody is going to hit you as hard as life but it ain't about how hard you get hit, it's about how hard you get hit and keep moving forward. That's how winning is done.

There are winners, there are losers and there are people that have not discovered how to win. You have gifts, don't keep them wrapped.

You are a good person. You will prevail and you're stronger than you think you are.

14

I'm not okay, you're not okay and it's okay

When you really think about it, what is okay? What is normal? You don't see dogs looking at other dogs thinking: 'That ain't normal' or cats looking at other cats going: 'That ain't normal.'

There's so much judgment out there. Then we judge ourselves, other people judge us and then we worry about other people judging us so it's okay to be not okay every once in a while.

How do I get better? As coach Kenny Lodato would say: 'If you're going to have an attitude, pick a good one.'

Somebody once told me that I have a chip on my shoulder. Yes, I do. When it comes to martial arts, fitness, yoga and nutrition, yes, I do. I've got 34 years in the bank, I've got a lot of flight time so you'd better believe I've got a chip on my shoulder. If that's not okay, I really don't care.

I'm not everybody's cup of tea, I really don't care. I'm at that age. In fact, I've been like that since I was in my 20s. If you don't like it, don't follow me, don't be friends with me. I'm not a politician, I'm a coach and I don't worry about everybody liking me.

Somebody told me I was aggressive. Yeah, I am aggressive. How do you think I built a business without being aggressive? And why is it all of a sudden seen as a bad thing? Why is it bad, being strong?

It's trial by fire. How are you going to know that person has your back if they haven't been through what you went through?

It's okay not to be okay. It's a dichotomy, it's black and white, it's left and right, it's up and down. Everything goes up, everything goes down. The tough part is taking a step back and just watching the cycles of your life.

As Dr Wayne Dyer would say: 'If you're in the valley, you should be celebrating because the hills are coming and you've got to move forward.'

What is behind me, it does not matter. It is only what is in front of me that matters. Go forward. Don't get stuck in the wake of your life.

I'm not okay, you're not okay and it's okay.

Different people see things differently. Dogs see light differently. I was over at my daughter's boyfriend's house, with the dog Luna and the cat. Luna gets pissed off when I'm patting the cat. 'Why is the cat getting all the attention?'

The dog tries to get the cat's attention and the cat looks up and goes whack with its paw. That's sometimes how you have to be.

I'm not okay, you're not okay and it's okay.

You need to figure out what success is for you. You need to figure out what homeostasis is for you, whatever that is. That's an even balance. Your balance is going to change from time to time. What was balance today may not be balance tomorrow. You have to be consistently inconsistent, you have to get comfortable with being uncomfortable because it happens. Every day is a little different. For me, it's like the weather. It's hot out there now and we were away a couple of weeks ago, and it was 48 degrees, but two days before that, it was 85.

Who knows? One of my famous sayings is: 'Life is an ocean.'

You're in your boat, nice and calm and then the next day or the next hour, you're battling for your life. You're getting thrashed around but that's what it is. Change is inevitable. Getting stuck where you are is a choice, so don't get stuck. Change is inevitable, especially if you live in the North East.

They say: 'If you don't like the weather, wait a minute.' If you're in England, wait a second because it changes so often.

I remember being in Chichester, doing certification. It was May or something, it was, like, 65, we're eating and as we came out of the restaurant, it snowed and hailed. 20 minutes later, the sun came out and it all melted.

I'm not okay, you're not okay and it's okay.

And what is okay? Is it the house, the car, the job, what is it? And at the end of the day, it is what it is.

You will figure it out, you always do. You always do, don't you? Look at the history. You've always figured it out, one way or the other. It may have taken you more time, more patience with yourself but you have figured it out. You always do. Trust in yourself. You've got this. You know you've got this.

You act like you. Go down swinging. You'll be okay for you, not for anybody else. You'll be okay for you. At the same time, be patient with yourself, pat yourself on the back, give yourself some honest appreciation for your journey because it is a journey. That's just the way it is.

It's like flying. Sometimes your radar isn't working so well and you're in the clouds, but the sun is always shining behind the clouds.

The sun is always shining behind the clouds. I'm not okay, you're not okay and it's okay. What is okay to you? What's your definition of okay? I know what mine is. Five or six hours of training a week, a set amount of money coming in, the kids being happy, blah, blah, blah. As long as there's joy, we're good. Just think about that.

I'm not okay, you're not okay and it's okay. What is okay to you?

It's just like success. What is success to you? More money? Great. Is it a better car? Being a good father, being a good coach, being a good friend and lover? Integrity, honor, character. That's what's important to me and that's success to me.

The rest of it, fine, I'll figure it out.

I do what I love and the money follows, it always has. Just like you should. Do what you love, the money will follow.

And don't forget, be relentless.

15

Don't sweat the small stuff and it's all small stuff

It's all small stuff. We make a big deal out of a ton of shit and it's a bunch of bullshit. I do it too.

The other day, I was driving to my older daughter's graduation and I was freaking out because I was late. I hit traffic and I was spasming, going ballistic. My younger daughter was sat there telling me to calm down and my older daughter was telling me that they probably locked the doors.

It was at that moment that I sat back and thought: 'There's no way they have locked the doors. Why would they lock the doors? We're going to get there. And from there on, that was my intention: to get there.

When I fly on planes, the way I think about it is: the plane will get there. Time moves forward. The plane will get there. And that's what you've got to do: just sit back, let life go and let it just happen. Don't sweat the small stuff.

Most of it is small stuff. 'I'm late for work, I'm late for my appointment'. What is it about being on time? You're late, so what? You're worried because it becomes a habit? You get fired and you have to figure it out and be on time from now on. It is what it is. Don't sweat the small stuff.

Will you look at this in five years? Probably not.

When I started my company, back in 1990, people were like: 'Oh, let's see what happens in five years.' Five years went by.

'Let's see what happens in 10 years.' Ten years went by. 'Let's see what happens in 15 years.' Fifteen years went by. It's now 34 years old. Drop the mic. Need I say fucking more? No.

Still doing it, still loving it, still doing everything I do because I don't sweat the small stuff. You never know when something's going to happen, something's going to change, when someone's going to say something or do something. You never know. The pain is temporary. Suffering is a choice, so don't sweat it.

The other day, I came home to a stimulus package and a check for $3000. Okay, I didn't expect it but I'll take the $3000. You just never know what's going to happen. It is what it is and I hate that saying it but it just is what it is.

I get things that stress me out, but then I just think: 'Screw it and do it.' Sometimes you've got to do it to get your point across: 'Fuck it.'

You want to ask that person out? You want to ask for a raise? Don't die wondering.

Most of the time we're so worried about what other people think of us when we do something, it's bullshit. If your heart tells you to do it, take good fucking note. When that speaks, listen, go with it. The opportunities that are here today may not be there tomorrow. That goes with business, relationships, it goes with love, it goes with all of it. Take the shot. Take the hill, just know what the hill is. Know what you want. It's what you have to have, what you must have.

I know what I want in business, I know the income I want to make, I know the person I want to have in my life. I found what I wanted with that. It took time, it took patience and I hope it goes for as long as it goes. I don't know what forever is, I'm just going to be in the moment with it and I'm not going to sweat the small stuff.

It is what it is, don't sweat the small stuff, just ride with it and have fun. Be
playful and don't worry about what other people think.

A few weeks ago, I did something and people were looking at me weirdly. 'What's the matter? Can't you let go? Can't you have fun? That's fine for you, but not me.'

I'm going to leave a legacy. I'm not going to die with my music in me. I won't sweat the small stuff. This is the key: dance like nobody is watching you, do your thing. Don't sweat the small stuff.

As Goggins would say: 'Fuck people.'

You want to judge me, fine, go ahead and judge me. Why don't you look in the mirror? There's a saying in al anon: 'Be careful pointing the finger because you've got three more pointing back at you.'

Judge other people? What gives you the right to do that? Judge yourself, look at yourself first, be honest with yourself. Ask yourself: what can I improve?

As Matthew McConaughey would say: 'Knowing who we are is hard. It's hard. So, give yourself a break. Eliminate who you are not, first. If you do that, you'll find yourself where you need to be.'

I know I'm not dishonest. I know I'm honorable. I know I have a high level of integrity. Know who you're not because knowing who you are is hard. It changes, it develops every day. We are always a work in progress. I know I am.

Don't sweat the small stuff, whatever it is.

Do you have credit card debt? It'll go away. Pay it off.

Did this happen, you got burned by this person? Did they break your heart? That's okay. Hearts were made to be mended.

You'll find somebody to fill in the cracks. You'll fill in your own cracks and then when you find that wow it will be all the more special because maybe that person who burned you taught you exactly what you wanted and you changed your standards.

I went through this crappy relationship. I thought this was the one and now I realize what I want. Now I realize I want this, this, this and this. I wanted this and now I've changed my standards.

Always move forward. Don't sweat the small stuff. Don't get stuck in the wake of your life that's been left behind the boat. You don't see a boat back up unless it's parking. It only goes forward.

Just keep going forward, don't sweat the small stuff. Will it matter in five or 10 years? Doubt it.

At the end of the day, try not to beat yourself up about it. Be honest with yourself but constantly hammering yourself is a virus of the mind. Somebody put it in your head that you're not good enough, that you're not smart enough, not sexy enough, whatever it is. It's all bullshit, complete bullshit, it's a virus of the mind. Don't listen to those people that kept chipping away at you, kept putting needles in your heart, like a pincushion. These people can't look honestly at themselves so they look at you, they point the finger at you. It's classic projection, so don't sweat it, just let it roll off you.

Be titanium and 10-feet tall because you are. If you've had kids, if you've gone beyond divorce, you are superhuman. Look back. You went through it, you were there. That calloused you. It's like working out in the gym, the first time it hurts but you've got to put the work in and then you get stronger, you get tougher, you get meaner and then you want it even more. Then you realize you're sore today, but you'll be fine tomorrow. You say: 'I'm going to go back, I'm going to hit it again, I'm going to hit it again.' Maybe I don't train that hard that day, maybe I go through the motions.

The fact that you showed up is 90 per cent of it. But remember, you can't crush it every day. Maybe not crushing it is crushing it. Ah, think about that. Maybe backing off is what you need to do. Sometimes you need to push forward, sometimes you need to step back. Sometimes you need to take two steps back to take one step forward. Sometimes you need to take four steps back to take one step forward or even half-a-step forward. The point of the matter is that you need to take the steps to greatness.

You are greatness, you will be greatness. Don't sweat the small stuff, it's all bullshit.

At the end of the day, don't do anything that degrades your soul or who you are, the core of your being.

Be relentless.

16

The hidden wound

I love superheroes and so do my children. I love comics. The movies. The epic battles between good and evil. My favorite superhero is Batman because when you get down to it, he actually doesn't have superpowers. Neither do I. Neither do you.

If I have a superpower, it would be the fact that I never give up. The villain that hunted me was depression. That was my enemy. I beat it by never fucking giving up.

I want to share my experiences so people suffering make superheroes of themselves. I want others in a fight with depression to learn this superpower.

Don't fight alone either. Seek out the other superheroes. The people who have struggled. The fighters who have overcome adversity. Fight this enemy together. That I can find support and strength in.

I like to surround myself with motivational messages. I've covered the walls in my home with posters and artworks. One of my favorites is an ancient ode of the Spartans.

'Make no mistake. I will defend the weak. I will defend my freedom. I will sacrifice so that others live free. I will defend my family to the death. I love peace but I am a fierce enemy. I live by a special code. I live with honor. I was born to be the warrior.'

Be a warrior. Fight through your struggles. Adversity is the calling of a warrior. It's not the size of the dog in the fight. It's the size of the fight in the dog.

I've had to fight for everything I have in my life. Talent never punched my ticket. I've been scratching and clawing all my life. All my successes have come as a result of my refusal to give up. It doesn't matter how often you get knocked down, so long as you keep getting up.

When I do speeches for school children about bullying, I always tell them that I'm not special. There is nothing special or exceptional about me. I'm just a man that never gave up.

The late, great Mohammed Ali said: 'Suffer now and live the rest of your life as a champion.' I think about that often.

You can't reach your goals and objectives without struggle. You have to fight.

If a client of mine is struggling with their training or not reaching their goals, I tell them about the Two Cs: commitment and consistency.

These two are inextricably linked, like the chicken and the egg. When you become consistent, you become committed. When you become committed, you become consistent.

After that, I tell them about the Three Ds which can be a recipe for success for anyone. Once you become committed and consistent, you get desire. You get dedication. You get discipline. It develops over time.

Do you want to be a duck or an eagle? Color outside the fucking lines. Fuck the lines altogether. Do you want to sit down there in the duck shit, or do you want to soar up there in the sky?

I take inspiration from punk rockers. Those guys with torn leather jackets and the mohawks. They're not normal and they don't care.

Don't be afraid to diverge from what people see as normal. It's okay to be unique. It's okay to be an individual. You may find that your greatest strengths lie in those divergences from the norm. In your eccentricities. Embrace it and learn how to draw power from it.

Be different. I'm not going to have a boring open casket when I die. Put me on a boat and sail me out to sea with my samurai sword and set me on fucking fire. I'm putting that in my will. Set me on fire like a fucking Viking.

I've always been a huge fan of Dr Wayne Dyer. One of my favorite quotes from him is: 'Hold your vision and keep your passion.'

This is key. If your passion wanes, you need to persevere. You need to invest in yourself. Find that willpower within.

When the depression had a hold of me, I wasn't coaching. I was having trouble with my children. My medication wasn't working. I got so low that I tried to slit my own throat.

Was this a selfish act? Yes. Undoubtedly. But that's how low I was. That's how far down the deep, dark hole I was.

I believe you can change the way your brain functions and operates. If you ever want to see this concept in action, then read Man's Search for Meaning by Victor Frankl. What he suffered through in that Nazi concentration camp was truly horrible but he stayed strong. They tortured him but they couldn't get to what was inside him.

Depression is a chemical problem but you can change it with the right tools. It's a matter of noticing the signs and triggers. From there, you need to try and channel it through the right avenues.

Exercise. Therapy. Meditation. Tai Chi. Whatever works for you. Don't give up. Don't fucking give up.

You're going to fail in life. No matter how hard you work in life, you're going to fail. Whether it's business or marriage, you're going to fail. You've got to get over it and move forward. That's all you can do.

I think of depression and anxiety as hidden wounds. It's a great concept because when you look at depression, anxiety and suicidal ideation and get down to it, you often don't see outward signs of mental illness in general. It really is a hidden wound. It's not a cast on your arm. If you're walking on a limp, people ask you what's wrong, what happened?

It's a hidden wound and nobody can see it. Nobody wants to talk about it. The stigma around mental health is bullshit. Absolute bullshit.

You're going to need friends to help heal this hidden wound. They may be people you don't even know yet. Reach out and seek support.

If you see a hidden wound in somebody you know, be a pest. Literally. Be a pest. You call them straight away. You show up at the door and ask them what's going on. Pester them.

I'd rather them hate me while they're alive and think I've overstepped my bounds than hate me dead. Don't be embarrassed about what people think. At least they'll be alive. They might hate you today. They might hate you tomorrow. But eventually they'll say: 'You know what, they saved my life.'

Winston Churchill said: 'Never give in. Never give in. Never, never, never, never—in nothing, great or small, large or petty— never give in, except to convictions of honor and good sense.'

I don't care what people think of me. I care about what I think about myself.

You put a lot of trust in people in the initial stages of a relationship. I had a girl move in with me a short while after we started dating. She wasn't on my lease. She wasn't paying rent.

When some friction started to emerge in the relationship, she tried to file a false domestic on me. It took me five days to get her out of my house.

It's important to look at your struggles and hardships as part of your life journey. I had to go through all that shit to get to where I am today. I could beat myself up that I wasted 20 years in a marriage but that was part of my life journey and I had to get through that to be the person that I wanted to be. I had to get through that to fall in love with the beautiful girl I'm with today.

You can't fucking give up. What gets you through the struggles and hardships is perseverance. Aim for the stars and if you don't quite hit them, you'll still be up there in the sky.

When I'm struggling, I like to think of a famous quote from Babe Ruth: 'Every strike brings me closer to my next home run.' You've just got to keep fucking swinging.

Depression is raw and real. It has a physical effect on you. It doesn't just affect your mind, it affects your whole body.

When I was going through the worst of it, I went in to take a shower one morning and just collapsed on the floor with an anxiety attack. It felt like I was having a heart attack. It came from nowhere.

It throws everything off balance, including your digestion. At times I swung from having the runs to constipation. At one stage, I wasn't able to take a shit for four days.

Forget about your sexuality. That's out the window too. Your libido disappears and if you do try, sometimes you can't even get it up.

The title of the book is a quote from my old therapist who helped me get through a really rough patch. She used to say that there was light in the tunnel, not just at the end of it. When you're in the grips of serious anxiety and depression you can't think about the end of the tunnel. You need to try and find a slither of light immediately.

When you're in the grips of depression, it's pitch black. You need to try and adjust your eyes and find some light there. Don't think about the end. Worry about the now. If you don't find a slither of light, you're going to die. Find that light.

Find the light in your life and win the fight against the hidden wound.

17

Being transparent is hard and necessary

When you become transparent, you really realize who your true friends are.

It's a concept I got from a client of mine that was going through similar shit that I went through.

I'm fortunate that I have a lot of close friends. Good friends are like stars: they drift apart, they come back. They're always there.

Mark DellaGrotte and I met at school in 1992. He went down the martial arts route, I went down the fitness route because I got my degree, and it is what it is.

He was out in the gutter, grinding it out, driving around on his motorcycle with his Thai pads. Mark wears his heart on his sleeve and so do I. People have told me for years, that I wear my heart on my sleeve and sometimes, when people say that, you wonder why they say that. Why are they bothering to say that? Is it a bad thing that I wear my heart on my sleeve? I've been called too sensitive. What the fuck is that? Really? What the fuck is that?

Is that something you say because it makes you feel better that you've said something that possibly insulted me? I've been called very sensitive; I've been called too sensitive but I like being that way. Mark DellaGrotte, same way. Joe Rogan, same way.

Mark shared a story with me the other day that he was at an investment meeting and there was a guy who was going to dump a bunch of money into his company and the guy didn't say anything for six hours. He was freaking out. He couldn't get a read of this guy and I'm the same way. I'd rather throw it all out there.

Just like that other client who's going through alcoholism with his wife and trying to go through recovery, you know who your true friends are.

If you say you have cancer, people show up at your door with plates of food but if you say you have mental illness, people won't touch you. It's frowned upon in this country and it's frowned upon in other countries.

So, when you become transparent, you know who your true friends are.

People say: 'Suck it up, eventually you'll get over it.' I come back to that with: 'You don't get to get over it, you have to learn to live with it and learn to manage it.'

I have a young client in his 30s, who comes from a lot of money. He's a good kid but he developed bad anxiety. But he got it. He got the whole gig of life. His father used to tell him to suck it up. Well, that really helped his relationship with his father. Is that his father's fault? No. No, it isn't. That's the way he was taught.

There is a story about a father who was at a party for someone and his son had died two weeks prior. He showed up at this party and people were like: 'What are you doing here? Your son…' And he said: 'I knew I had to get over it sometime.' Do you get over it? I don't think you do. I think you learn to live with it.

It's kind of like mental illness, you learn to live with it. You decide to be cured, you learn the signs and symptoms of going off track, of going off the rails and your good friends will still be there. Good friends will be there to help you get your shit together, to ask you what's happening, what's going on, to ask you what's going on with your life or how you're feeling. Just like the beautiful people at McLean. Every time I'd go in to ECT, I'd be asked how I was feeling.

Good friends… You want to talk about good friends? Craig

Rose and his wife would come down from Linfield on his day off to pick me up and take me to ECT because I couldn't drive. They knock you out. It's a 30-minute procedure with a long recovery cycle. It takes four hours by the time you recover and then you can't drive and then you're supposedly going to have somebody with you. Yeah, that didn't work. How am I going to have somebody stay with me when they just blew up half their day? Think about that, true friends and true family don't judge.

If I hurt my eye, people would be like: 'Oh, how you been?' 'Are you okay?' But if I have something going on in my brain, it's: 'Let's stay away from him.' That's why, in the dating world, I end up dumping them after the second or third date.

Coach Corey Wayne says people have to get their baggage up. No, not all of their baggage but a fair part of it. That's because if I'm going to go full with somebody and they're gonna judge me for trying to take my own life, it's not going to work. Given the set of circumstances, they haven't walked in my shoes, they haven't lived the way I lived and, you know what, just fuck off. And I don't mean that in a derogatory way, I mean it in a nice way. 'Okay, fine, if you can't deal with it, move on. And you've got your own shit to deal with.'

When I first came out into the dating world, people were telling me that I was in great shape and that I should go for somebody in their 30s. No fucking way. They haven't figured out life and the sad part is that there are people in their 40s and 50s that are drowning their shit in alcohol, drugs and work.

I don't drown myself in work. I know when to shut it off and shut it down. Am I a nut bag? Fuck, yeah. ABC, man. Always be closing.

Good friends are like stars. People that I haven't seen for a long time, they find out that I just tried to take my own life and they ask: 'What, you?'

I'm like: 'Yeah, because I have the appearance of having it all together.'

I'm cranking it out. At one point, I was training 15 UFC fighters, the whole nine yards and inside I was fucking dying, just dying.

My marriage was falling apart, I was having financial trouble, the whole bit and I just kept trying to move forward. I have my own demons, we all have our own fucking demons and anybody who says they don't, they're doing something else — eating, drinking, smoking, sex addiction, whatever it is — to compensate.

I think everybody has some form of addiction. Me? I'm addicted to martial arts. Am I addicted to fitness? Absolutely. Am I addicted to Burn With Kearns? Absolutely. Why? Because of my brand and the training methodologies. Am I addicted to yoga? Yeah. Now, healthy addictions are okay.

Obsession addiction is a different story. I don't obsess about exercise. One thing that yoga taught me is that there's a time for being rigorous and a time for rest, kind of like yin and yang.

People don't grasp the concept of the yin and yang symbol. You've got black with white and you've got white with black. What does that mean? Strength. Soft and hard. People think that Muay Thai is all hard style, it's not. You look at Tony Jaa when he was trained by the Grandmaster, that wasn't hard style, that was fluidity.

Good friends are important, man... Be transparent.

Some people spout off because of my Coffee With Coach because I do this and that. Fuck you, just fuck you. Somebody told me that I could get an infomercial but I was going to have to change my syntax. They said they would have to get me a speech coach.

Really? Did fucking Arnold Schwarzenegger get a speech coach? Please. The first thing he got told was that his name was too long and that nobody could understand him. Boom. He still made it, he's one of the most successful actors there is. What else did he do? He ran for governor and won. At the end of the day, the guy's been hitting the net for 40 years because he said: 'Screw you'. I remember the guy who directed *Conan The Barbarian*, Arnold's first big role, saying that they would have had to have made *Conan* if they didn't have Arnold.

You've got to swing for the fence, man. Be transparent. Wear your heart on your sleeve. If one door closes, there's always going to be another door. Me? Fuck the door, I'm going to kick the fucking thing in. Watch me.

It's okay to be an underdog, okay to fail, okay to fall flat on your face, okay to cry, okay to be sad. You think I'm happy all the time? No. I have my moments and I move on. You can have your moment and then you have to get back to work. You're going to pull yourself up by your bootstraps and get back to work.

What's your mission? What's your how? What's the what? What's the why? Why are you doing what you're doing?

I don't want to hear: 'I'm too old' or 'I'm too fat'. Shut the fuck up. Just shut up. Stop complaining and start training.

Do you think I wasn't scared the first time I was at the Idea World Fitness Show and there's 200 people, all basically colleagues, that are looking at me, just waiting at me to fucking fail, just so they could say that was shit? Why? Because people are negative sometimes.

Douglas Brooks walked into my seminar 45 minutes into it. He spent two-and-a-half hours on the phone to me 30 years before because I wrote him a letter after reading his book. A letter about how to build my business and whatever. He spent two-and-a-half hours on the phone to me one night, he didn't even know me from Adam and I said: 'Never underestimate the power of kindness.'

What does he do? He sees me and he gives me the thumbs up. So, I introduce him and say: 'That's the man, the main reason why I'm here.' Pay it forward, pay it forward.

Real friends. Good friends, solid friends, they have your back. They might yell at you, they might give you shit, they might call you out but at the end of the day, they're still there. They've still got your back and sometimes you need a fucking smack on the head. I do, every once in a while.

I got that smack on the head recently, when my daughter's birthday was coming up. We share custody 50 per cent and it's the kids' choice. I'm like: 'Argh'. My friend Chris Foamer told me to reach out to her and I'd already sent her a gift. He said: 'No, reach out to her and tell her that you'd like to see her on her birthday.'

I wouldn't want to fucking do that because I was afraid of failing and then I said: 'Fuck it. You know what, you're right.'

I'll tell somebody they're right but don't tell me I'm right.

I want to tell the truth and I want to be effective, that's my goal. I don't want to be right. I'm not

trying to one-up you. I can't stand when people one-up and try to keep score.

Mike and I have known each other since fucking '92. Do you think we keep score of all the shit we've done together? All the fights we've had, all the blood, sweat and tears.

Coach Steve Whittier and I, do you think we keep fucking score? Lionel Beane, I've known since we were 13.

Craig Rose, I've known since I was 16. Do you think we keep score? I don't fucking keep score. Jamie Burke, you think I keep score? No.

Close friends don't keep score.

Family gets a little fucking whack, whack. True friends are there.

'I love you, bro…' When Mark and I say that to each other, we mean it. Steve Whittier and I say it to each other and we mean it. Craig Rose, Lionel Beane, all the others, those are different stories. Those are different stories because we mean it. We'll lay down in fucking traffic for anybody.

True friends have your back, true friends have your six, that's when you go into combat. That's one thing I wish I'd done is military. When you go into combat, it's a brotherhood.

When you're the first law enforcement officer in a room after the battering ram, you know that your fellow officers have your back. That's what friendship should be: a brotherhood, a band of brothers or sisters or whatever you want to call it.

Be transparent. Your true friends, you'll know who they are because they're like stars. They're always going to be there. I just reached out to a friend of mine, Wendell Taylor. I started at the same time he started. 'What up, bro?' I hadn't seen him in 10 years.

Professor Tim Brill reached out to me last week wanting to apologize for not doing the work on a seminar he hosted for me back in 2008. I hadn't spoken to him in, like, 12 years. 'I know,' he said. 'But I just felt bad.' I told him he was forgiven. Not that there was anything to forgive him for.

You do it because you want to do it, not because you have to do it. You and your true friends shouldn't keep score. You shouldn't do something because you have an ulterior motive or because you're playing chess with them. You don't play chess, you play checkers. 'Got you on that one, let's move on.'

Better yet, you can be a doer for your true friends. They don't want you to do something for them so you say: 'No, fuck you, I'm doing this for you and if you want to argue with me, we'll go outside. Let's go outside.'

I take a page from the Mandalorian: 'I have spoken, and this is the way it is.'

Being friends with people is like being a coach. You've got to know when to hold them, when to use kid gloves and know when to smack him upside the head. 'What the fuck are you doing? Get your shit together, stop the pity party.' The pity party can only last so long.

Take the book *29 Gifts* for example, the woman had MS and cured herself by giving stuff away. What about Jim Derrick? 10 or 15 years ago he was diagnosed with MS. They said he was going to be in a wheelchair, and he was like: 'Fuck you'. You look at people like J-Rob who was diagnosed with type two diabetes in, like, '78. He was like: 'Fuck you' when they suggested treatment. He did it with just food and exercise. The guy's, like, 60 and looks about freaking 30. He's got the whole hippie lifestyle. He's a surfer guy, he has a successful company, JRR Protein Powder, for the whole nine yards. He cured himself with food and exercise because he was transparent.

As Matthew McConaughey would say: 'Whatever your answer is, don't choose anything that will jeopardize your soul. Prioritize who you are, who you want to be and don't spend time with anything that antagonizes your character.'

You can have your full wallet, you can have your big fucking house, you can be flying here, flying there but at the end of the day, when you die, you'll be alone and you can't take all that with you.

An honest man's pillow is his peace of mind and when you lay down on the pillow at night, no matter who's in our bed we all sleep alone.

I have no trouble when my head hits that pillow and if I fuck up, I fucking fix it. I'll own it.

What I don't like is when it's not brought to my attention. If you don't tell me, I can't fix it. I'm fucking human, I'm fallible. I'm not perfect and that's what going through mental illness taught me, as did going through attempted suicide.

I'm not perfect. Shit happens. I get overwhelmed, I can admit it. Everybody gets overwhelmed, that's why you reach out to a hotline, you reach out to a third person, you reach out to your friends, somebody you can trust, a mentor.

Good friends are like stars: you may not always see them but they're always there. Live it, learn it, do it.

18

Keep moving forward

Let's talk a little bit about business or branding. Whatever business you're in, whether you're a hygienist, doctor, it doesn't matter what you are, you have to have your own brand. I built my own brand for years and I'm on the verge of signing a deal that I've already had blow over my face twice. I just keep moving forward.

There are a lot of great books out there and suggestions, and one of the best books that I've ever read was *How To Win Friends & Influence People* by Dale Carnegie. People criticize his techniques and call them a form of manipulation but it really isn't because the three fundamentals are: don't criticize, condemn or complain. He teaches people to show honest, sincere appreciation and be genuinely interested in others.

When you think about that, it is really important.

A little gem of wisdom from David Goggins is that you can't give a fuck what other people think. The more successful you are, the more you're going to have haters because they can't do it, because they're part of the 99 per cent that won't do it.

David Goggins also said: 'The mind's tired but the body isn't.'

A human being can be anything. A dog can only be a dog, a squirrel can only be a squirrel, a tree can only be a tree but you can be anything you want and if you want it then you have to go out there and take it.

One of the key points of Dale Carnegie's book is to call people by their names. I have doormen in Vegas that are now my friends because when I was doing the fights, I would call them by their names. I still have their emails.

It's a sphere of influence, that's what you want. I've had people try to intimidate me and manipulate me but I'm a street kid and sooner or later, you figure it out. We're not dumb, we know the angles. I don't need a 4.0 to know that somebody's jerking me around. People have called me Dalton from *Roadhouse*. 'Be nice until it's time not to be nice.'

Fill your mind with inspiration, change your thoughts and your ways. Read anything from Zig Ziglar, Roger Dawson and Dr Wayne Dyer. Richard Carlson's *Don't Sweat The Small Stuff & It's All Small Stuff* is an amazing book because it really is all small stuff.

There is no yellow brick road, there is no easy, simple way to do anything. Life's hard. It wasn't meant to be easy. On one side of the coin you have acts of human kindness and empathy and on the other you have evil and treachery. People are complicated and people do silly, stupid things. They're very self- centered and have a lack of personal responsibility. That's what it boils down to: a lack of personal responsibility and I can't stand that.

Own your shit and if you're going to talk the talk, walk the walk. Plain and simple, own your shit. Maybe that is going to be my next book. Most people nowadays are about not owning their shit. Most people nowadays want to post something on Facebook or Instagram, all this fucking bullshit.

Get it done, under the sun and if there's no sun then make your own sun because at the end of the day, you are the sun. Remember that you are definitely the sun. Don't quit, don't stop. Don't stop 'til you get enough, just like in the old Michael Jackson song. Just keep going. Read, listen and learn. Always be a white belt, never stop moving forward, never look back. Fuck the past, it doesn't matter.

Keep moving forward. You can do it.

Be relentless.

19

The act of giving

One thing I want to talk about is the act of giving.

They've proven that when you give somebody something, it not only raises the serotonin levels of the receiver and the giver but the people witnessing it.

Being a human being is hard. You have to pay the mortgage, get a credit card, send your kids to college and all the rest of it.

Take a dog, for example. They wake up, think: 'I'm going to eat' and you tell them it's not 6am. What do you know? You're supposed to eat at six. They don't have a clock, they're not using their fucking Apple Watch.

It's the same for us. If you give a smile to somebody, most of the time you never know what you're going to say or do.

I'm a name badge freak and I learned that from Dale Carnegie. I'll call people by their name and it just softens them. Most of the time, they're being called 'you' or 'buddy' or it's 'Hey sir,' or 'Hey miss' and I don't know about you, but I don't want to be addressed that way.

The funniest thing I've ever seen is when some people at the seminars I was doing would call me 'Mr. Burns.'

I'm like: 'Mr. Burns? Well, where's Kearns?' I just play around with it and let them go.

I'm not a big fan of tearing people down. I'm always a big fan of propping people up and I can't stand it when I see people putting people down, even if it's in the movies.

How can you not like golden retrievers? We should all have the golden retriever personality, we should all have the golden retriever mentality: just chill, lay down, feed me, pat me, the whole nine yards.

Life would be so easy if we were all like dogs. They're like: 'Yeah, I think we're going over here.' He's not worried about how he looks, he's not worried about how his coat needs to be, how he needs to be brushed. He's not worried about taking a dump and everybody watching him, he's not worried about taking a piss anywhere he wants. He just pees. He just does his thing and you should also just do your thing and not be afraid to give somebody something, a smile, a wink, a nod.

I always remember the scene in *Crocodile Dundee* where Paul Hogan is walking through New York. 'Good day, good day, good day, good day, good day.' He's just saying hello to everybody he meets as he's walking to the train and people get all wound up because they don't know the person and they assume that they want something. 'I don't want anything, I'm just saying: 'Hi, how you doing.'

If you don't have any money to give, give somebody a smile, give somebody a look, tell somebody a joke, see how they are.

One of the things I like doing is asking somebody their name. 'Hey man, you definitely look like a Kenneth'. Or: 'You definitely look like a Tara' or whatever it is.

When I'm in a restaurant and see a kid aged between 16 and 20, running around, busting their ass, bussing tables I'll be like: 'Excuse me, what's your name and how old are you?'

One guy who friended me on Facebook told me that he was just 17 and I said to him: 'You know, you could be home, playing video games on this nice day or you could be doing something else but you're bussing.'

He told me that he had to work so, in an affluent neighborhood, I turned around and gave him $20.

He was like: 'Are you sure?'

I said: 'Yeah, man, you do a good job.'

I like to see that strong work ethic. Why not prop people up?

When I was in Starbucks in a wealthy area during the pandemic somebody pointed out that the tip cup was empty.

I was like: 'Really? Range Rovers and Audis were parked up and nobody gave in the tip cup.'

I walked over and threw in 100 bucks. I grabbed hold of the manager and told him that I respected him because he was doing a good job and that's how you reward people.

That hundred bucks meant a lot to me but it meant a lot more to everybody behind the desk, everyone busting their ass behind the counter.

So, think about that. Think about trying to raise the serotonin levels of somebody else. If they don't accept it, so what? At least you tried. You took care of your side of the street. Your side of the street is clean.

Please, be relentless.

20

Be relentless

I want to talk about the concept of the tattoo that I got on the left center of my chest recently.

'Be relentless.' What is that about?

Well, let me tell you. When you're self-employed, you have to be relentless. You just do. The average person will just give up. You have to be extremely passionate about what you do, extremely passionate about feeling better.

If you haven't found your passion, that's okay. Look for it and keep looking for it. It will happen. You'll find that thing.

My youngest daughter just said that she wants to go to college to become a medic. I was like 'Great.'

'Are you okay with that?'

'Absolutely, honey,' I replied. 'As long as it makes you happy and brings you joy. How many people go to work and fucking hate their jobs?

There are parts of my job that I extremely dislike, like traffic — and you can't even time it because everybody's telecommuting. There can be difficult customers and you have to ask yourself how you can work around these things, how you can manage them. That's how you learn.

A mistake is only a mistake if you don't learn the lesson because most of the time there is a lesson to be learned.

How do you know what sharpness is until you cut yourself? How do you know what hot is until you burn yourself? How do you know what failure is until you fall flat on your face?

That's okay. You get knocked down, you get up.

Equate it to when you were two years old or however old you were and you were learning to walk. When you fell down, you get right back up. Take it from someone who was last able to tie his sneakers, last to take the training wheels off his bike, it was embarrassing as fuck. But I didn't know any better.

The story that you believe — even at six and seven — is that everyone is looking at you for your failures and will be telling you that you suck, even though it's not true. It's a story that you believe, though, because somebody put it in your head. It's called a virus of the mind.

'You'll never amount to anything, you'll never do anything, blah, blah, blah, blah, blah.'

A lot of the time when people point the finger, they forget that there are three more pointing back at them.

You want to judge? Go ahead, I really don't give a fuck. Go ahead and judge me. I did this, did I do that? Yeah, I did.

I went out with a friend, not so long ago, and they were like: 'You got me drunk' and I was like: 'Yes — and I take full responsibility.' I'm a bad influence, a bad seed. So you got drunk, big deal.

How do you know how to not have a hangover until you've got one? 'Ah, man, I'm never drinking again…'

Been there, done that. That happens, you're hugging the toilet bowl, but what do you do? You can still drink again. But after a while you get smarter.

Me? If I have a little bit too much, I have at least a liter, if not two liters of water before I go to bed. Boom. I drink myself straight, straight as an arrow. At the end of the day, it doesn't matter. So what? You drank too much or you ate too much… So what? Just don't keep doing it.

If it doesn't feed your soul, don't do it.

Do it. What are you waiting for? No regrets. I'd rather regret the things I did do than the things I didn't do. I'd rather work and not make it and fail, just to know that I did it. At least you did it and then you're refining the process.

You've got to put what you want out there in the universe. You've got to talk about it, be loud and proud and that's just the way it is.

When Jim Carey did *Cable Guy*, he made the biggest payday ever — $21 million — and that was after his agent told him to write out a check for what he wanted to be paid because he was upset that he wasn't getting paid enough. He posted it to his mirror and a year after writing that check, Jim Carey landed the part in Ace Ventura for $996,000.

More money is good but there's a certain point where you kind of go: 'Okay, that's enough.'

Amazon CEO Jeff Bezos is going to be the first trillionaire. Does he really need it? How many trains, planes and automobiles does he need?

Me? I want to have fun. I want to be healthy. I want healthy relationships, I want to be healthy in myself and I want a good business. That's my pyramid.

When you look at it, my father died at 48. It wasn't his fault but he chose not to stay healthy. I chose to stay healthy, I didn't want my kids growing up without a father.

It's not that it was bad for me, it was rough but it taught me a lot about myself. The death of my father taught me self-alliance, taught me tenacity. I really got the idea that you have to be relentless.

I'm relentless in business and people say to me: 'Why don't you just chill?'

I'm like: 'No, I'm not going to fucking chill out.' That's because I want to get it done — and it will get done. Sometimes I'll relax but it's still cooking in the brain.

People say I'm a multi-tasker. No, not really. Do you know what I am? I'm a chef. I've got six or seven burners going and I'm just moving shit around.

'Hey, that's done, that's got to be moved forward. That's done, that's done, that sauce is almost ready.' That's what you do. You spin the plates, you just watch. 'Where do I have to go next? What do I have to do next? Is this going to fall? Is that going to fall?'

You have to play the game.

It's a lot like martial arts, you have to adapt and overcome. That's what's great about human beings, we can adapt and overcome. Just look what we've done. We started off as monkeys and then we adapted and overcame and now we build bridges, we build skyscrapers, we have phones, we have cars, we can record shit.

A human being can be anything it wants. You can be anything you want. The only gifts that you can give people who are in your inner circle are your time, your attention and your patience but you can't do that if you don't take any time for yourself. Your honor, your loyalty and your integrity can be given too but most importantly, it's your time and attention.

It's something that everybody needs. Not just for those close to you, but for yourself, too.

21

How do you want your life to look?

You've been through a lot, you're going through a lot, I get it. You've been there, done that.

Me, I want to leave a legacy. I want to know I've been a good father, I want to know I was a good partner, I want to know I was a good coach and I want to know that I helped some people.

I was on a program called *Pressing the Limits* with Jon Bruney and John Brookfield and Bruney started the conversation with: 'In the fitness industry, in MMA, when you hear the name Kevin Kearns, everybody knows who you are'.

I was completely flabbergasted and thrown aback. I was like: 'Wow, man, I don't know what to say to that.'

Here's a guy that has umpteen records and he's telling me that everybody knows me? At the end of the day, I try to do a good job, write a good article, do a good video, sell a good product, try to help some people, try to make them happy. I want to be the one to say: 'Hey, man. You can do it.'

Prop people up and push them. Years ago, we used to say: '10 fingers and a boost.' Give people a boost. At the end of the day, no matter what you do in your job, just give them a boost. I'm not saying go home with them, just give them a boost.

There was a great chapter in one of my daughter's books — I think it was a Barbie book — and it was about being scared to go to a party. Maybe you're going to meet a friend you've never met before. How do you know someone is going to be your friend until you meet them?

How do you know, if you don't ask that woman or guy out, that they're not going to be the person for you? That they're not going to be the wow that you've been looking for. How do you know that? You don't know that. Take the shot. Why not? Fuck it.

If you aim for the moon and you miss it, you'll land among the stars and that's the way it is. Swing for the fence because at the end of the day, it doesn't matter.

Look at all the sports stars, a football player's average career is two to three years. That's a short window, man. A short window. You get one life to live so live it.

Carpe diem, seize the day.

Don't take care because people who take care don't get anywhere. Take charge and move forward.

22

The final chapter

I wanted this book to come out six months ago and lots of people want a lot of things. It is what it is, right? Things happen, maybe for a reason, and I believe that 100 per cent.

So, I've decided that this is going to be the final chapter of my new book: *There's Light in The Tunnel: How to Survive & Thrive With Depression.*

Be relentless. It's one of my favorite things to say. And what that means is just don't fucking quit.

Fuck what other people think, fuck that shit. Find out what you want and just keep going. I know it sucks, I know it's hard and I know you feel like there's no way out but there is a way out.

Pull yourself up. You'll have your moments but don't judge. 'It took me this long to do this, it took me this long to do that... 'Well, I can flip the script on that. How long did it take you to ride a fucking bike? How long did it take you to learn how to drive, to kiss a girl the right way, to kiss a boy the right way? How long did it take you to get where you wanted in your career?

You can judge but at the end of the day, it's a waste of fucking time and energy. I've been there and done that. I beat myself up more than anybody when I do something wrong or incorrect, when I fuck up. Everybody fucks up. But you get out there. You're in the dating world in your 40s and 50s and everybody's got challenges, everybody's has trauma. You've got to feel it out which isn't simple. Often people that have gone down this path and gotten into deep depression are empathetic and sensitive. These qualities are gifts but can also be a curse.

'You're too sensitive, you're too empathetic,' that's fucking bullshit. Any time they put an adjective in front of something else that's a negative, fuck them.

I've been called too sensitive, but I'll correct you. I'm sensitive and I'm sensitive because it makes me a good coach, a good human being and a good father. What do you want? Do you want to be the Terminator, to be insensitive, an arsehole? So, what if I wear my heart on my sleeve? Big deal. Maybe I'm different to you because you have no empathy and sensitivity. That might be because you're a narcissist who only gives a shit about themselves.

Never mind: 'What can I get?' How about: 'What can I do for other people?' How about giving versus just receiving, huh?

My concept of being relentless is being non-stop. I've been called aggressive. How do you think I built a business without being aggressive? And why is it all of a sudden seen as a bad thing? Why is it bad, being strong? It doesn't mean I want to go and rip people's throats out. It means I'm aggressive, I move forward, I don't stop. If I get knocked down, I get back up.

Being depressed and being on the verge of the abyss and trying to commit suicide is a fucking journey, man, and it sucks. I'm not gonna lie to you, it sucks. Every fall from grace will bring you higher. The harder the struggle, the more the rebound, the bigger the bounce. Then you can get right with it, you can reflect back and ask yourself how you got there.

You've got to be relentless, you've got to get that fire back and yeah, I get it, bad marriage, bad relationship, work environment, COVID, all of it, it sucks.

You get divorced and it's the death of a marriage, the death of a relationship, shit goes sideways, you get manipulated and it's all about them or it's all about you or whatever it is and it never ends well.

I have a close friend who had an amicable divorce and he still had to go to therapy.

I've had a lot of clients go through the whole divorce process and everybody said it takes two to three years to get back to normal. I didn't realize that. It's true but as much as you need to walk away from the person, it's going be hard on you and hard on your family. You're breaking up the family unit and if you're in my age group, you are taught: 'Until death do us part' and: 'In sickness and in health.'

And if there's alcoholism or some other type of bullshit behavior, whatever it is, you figure that you hang in there, you hang in there and then you sit there and you reflect and you go: 'Well, I hung in for the kids, the house, the equity line, the IRA, all the other bullshit...'

At the end of the day, did it help? I had somebody advise me to wait until the kids were in college. Why should I? So, I'm gonna show them the wrong way a relationship should work? Fuck that. It shouldn't be controlling and manipulative and condescending and you shouldn't be getting put down and bullied. I don't want to show my kids that.

This is not going to be easy for anybody and you know what, I really don't give a fuck. I really don't care. We went through what we went through. I know the truth and I know the facts.

You've got to be relentless and you've got to be relentless with yourself. Choose the right support staff. If your significant other or your family aren't supporting you in the right way, you need to talk to them and if they're still hammering you, you drop them off a cliff. That's it.

Because what gives them the right, just because they're tied to you by blood, to say anything derogatory towards you?

You find your closest friends and they'll tell you what you need to know.

I had to cut somebody off that I had known for more than 30 years because I was in a rough place a year ago when I was dating somebody that was not good for me. She kept calling me self-centered and selfish and the whole nine yards. I'm six months out from trying to commit suicide and I tried to call a couple of people. I got a hold of somebody who I thought was a close friend and we're going back and forth a little bit and then from out of nowhere he says to me: 'You're the most self-centered person I've ever met in my life.' I'd known him since I was 15. I tapped the brakes, hung up and cut him off.

When somebody says something like that, there's a lot of projection there because that's how they felt at that point in their life. Are they going to judge me? No. Look in the fucking mirror, look at yourself.

At the end of the day, it's real simple. You fuck up, you own it, you do your best to fix it and you move on.

I'm the worst for it, I can't stand watching videos of myself, I rip myself apart, I beat myself up. It's a dichotomy. Some of that's good and it keeps you grounded because you can pull the weeds out daily and by the same token it's just not good for yourself. You've gotta sit there and figure out the best way to handle it.

Being relentless is different. It just means that you have to find that thread that you can pull on for yourself. What do you want to do? I'm fortunate that I've helped 10-12 people not commit suicide. I've helped them get the help they need over the past year because I came out.

As David Goggins would say, just me talking about it makes me feel better. Sometimes, in fact all the time, that's what you need to do. You need to talk about it.

Going into relationships, it's really simple. Here are my rules, my foundations: honest appreciation, honest affection, honest communication and loyalty. That's all I ask for. They're not really rules, they're just standards. As you get further and further on in life, you raise your standards. Whether that be your career, your job, your relationship, your intimate relations, you raise your standards. 'No, I'm not going to accept that.' And at the same time, you realize you are fallible. That was one of the hardest things. I was so busy being Coach Kearns that it crept up on me. Before I knew it, my ego had taken over in my head. 'I can handle this, I'm Coach Kearns, I'm stronger than this, I'm Batman, blah, blah, blah...' and I couldn't handle it. I fucked up. I'm going to say that to be honest and I'm not gonna torture myself at the same time. I've already done that, I've tortured myself enough over this.

My kids moved out over 18 months ago because my ex used my mental illness and my mental challenges against me to convince them to move out. It led to me attempting suicide because it just broke me. I look back at the six or seven months we had to live together after the divorce and it was brutal. I blocked it out. I don't remember Thanksgiving or Christmas. I don't remember any of it, I just blocked it out. Now my youngest is back with me and I'm very thankful.

When two people are living in the same house that they don't want to be with each other, that have broken that commitment off, that they basically don't want to be around each other, it's brutal. But all the lawyers and everyone were saying that we had to stay. I wanted to move out right away and get as far away from her as possible. Break the contact, break it off, move on and just get the fuck out of dodge. Unfortunately, we had to stay because that was the best thing for the legal process and the money and all that other bullshit.

At the end of the day, you have to sit there and maintain being relentless. You'll find yourself- respect, you'll find your self-discipline and self-discipline is self-love.

Eat healthy food, get enough sleep, do what you enjoy doing. If people aren't on your support team, drop them. Sometimes people will flip the script and change the gears. Be patient with yourself. It's difficult and I know it's hard but own your shit and don't blame yourself.

I don't care about being right, I'm all about telling the truth and being effective. Every relationship is an opportunity for growth for both people. Learn something.

They say people don't change. That's bullshit. People change, trauma happens. Look at the whole in vitro process. I've been through it. It sucks. You're pregnant, you're not pregnant. It's not bad, it's not good, it's just an experience.

At the end of the day, be relentless. Push forward.

I want to end with some pearls of wisdom and one of my favorite sayings is: 'Yesterday is history, tomorrow is a mystery. Today is a gift and that's why it's called the present.'

My father, God rest his soul, and my mother, would take pictures when we went on holiday and then once a month he would have a slideshow. We had the projector and we would put up a screen. We had popcorn and it was like watching a movie. We had a slideshow about where we'd been and what we'd done. Pictures have energy. You know the best thing about smartphones?

You can take pictures and memories so easily and effortlessly.

Things like that, you kind of forget. Create memories that matter. Moments matter. Even the rough moments matter.

The first time I was getting wheeled down to ECT therapy, I was scared shitless but I knew in my heart that it was the right decision. I knew I had to do it and after three treatments I felt a lot better. I took a shot. I took a chance. I took a shot and I went for it. Just like that.

Do you think I want to talk about my illness, about falling down, about my blackest of black, just like when I had to talk about my bullying and how I got bullied even more as I got older?

Shit happens, people change and you can change. If everybody was the same, this whole planet would be boring as fuck. Imagine if we had no emotion, no feeling, no nothing. People are different and that's the fun part. Black, white, Hispanic, it doesn't matter. Men, women, whatever it is. We're all different. That's the joy of it. There's respect and honor in that. We should honor our differences.

You're an influencer and your friends and your kids and people that you influence will pick things up from you. Even if you're not out there in the public eye, you're an influencer. Your whole point is to be a good influence on your kids, to help them mediate what comes down the pipe.

If you have kids, if you're a mother or a father, you're superhuman. You'll try your best to make it work. You'll take all the brunt of the pain but at the end of the day, the kids are going to feel some pain, they have to.

Pain is inevitable, suffering is a choice. Remember that. Honest pain is okay. You hurt somebody's feelings? You feel fucked up about it and you apologize, and you give maximum effort.

You go down, you lay your heart on the table and you look them dead in the eye and you say you're sorry. How can I fix it? How can I make this better? Own your shit.

Always be a white belt. Always be learning, whether it's business, martial arts, fitness or relationships, always be learning.

Always be willing to learn.

Like one of my big clients and mentors, Phil Healey would say: 'Look for the interesting things in this world.' I find everything interesting. I find human interaction interesting. I find nature interesting. I find training interesting. I am a scientist. It's interesting that what's here today might be different tomorrow.

Don't criticize, condemn or complain, be genuinely interested in people and remember to show honest, sincere appreciation.

Make other people's day and when you're having a rough time, reach out to your support staff. Your close-range support staff are people that are close to your heart, close to your soul. You keep them close. Those are your first barriers, your first go-to.

Unwrap your gifts because everybody's got them, whether it's being empathetic or being a motivator.

I'm lucky, I get to do it every day. Sometimes it's challenging to establish a rapport with people, to make them feel good and to push them forward. I might be in a room with 10-20 police officers, or I may be in the room with 200 trainers and they're all like: 'Who's this guy, Mr UFC trainer?'

You've just got to let go and let God guide you. Swing for the fence. Fuck it. Just do it. No risk, no reward.

Love's a risk, getting up in the morning is a risk, driving's a risk, work's a risk. They tell you that sitting out in the sun's a risk but I'm still going to sit in the sun.

Walking the river is a risk. At the end of the day, life is full of risks. If you want to be fucking bubble boy, stay in a fucking bubble man.

I'm not staying in a bubble, though. Those important to me know how I am. I'll take the first hit. I'll take the second hit. My sword and my shield are yours. If it's anybody close to me, in my close- range circle, I'll take the shot.

You want me to hold your hand next to you while they come at you, fine. I'll stand in the fire, I don't give a shit. I like the heat. Bring it, fuck them.

Every soldier needs a moment. Every soldier needs a moment. Every warrior needs a moment and we're all fucking warriors. Remember that. We're all fucking warriors. Yeah, I'm dropping those bombs and I really don't give a shit.

Like David Goggins said: 'The further you go up the ladder, you're gonna have haters.' I've got plenty of haters. People rip me apart every day and you know what? Go fuck yourself. You know why? Because I'm always a white belt. I'm always performing, I'm always perfecting my whole thing and there is no perfection. It's progress, not perfection and we are all in progress.

At the end of the day, all I want is for people to call me a mensch. I'm a good man. I know plenty of men out there who suck. Yeah, you suck, because you think with the little head and not the big head. You don't think with your heart. You're afraid to be vulnerable because basically you're a pansy.

I have a saying… 'First time, my mistake. Second time, my mom made a mistake for not teaching me better. Third time, you must just like it.'

You must just like it. You've got to look in the mirror and look at yourself. Self-responsibility and personal responsibility are lacking in this world. When I make a mistake, I beat myself up for days. I'm getting better at it but even if I apologize and make amends, I'll still beat myself up about it. I'll figure it out and I'll get through it and that's just me.

And, you know, it's just you.

Some people get aggravated when they drive, it's all an experience. Some people take 20 minutes to order food. So what? I'm not in a rush. Even if I'm starving and that person's taking 20 minutes to order food, that's okay because they're just checking out their options. It's not that you can't make a decision because if you couldn't make a decision you would never have come into the restaurant. You would never have got up. You wouldn't have gone to work. Some people take more time, they evaluate options. Me? What do I do? Sometimes I don't laser focus and I pull the trigger and then when I reflect, I think: 'Fuck'. But then I judge that I shouldn't have done it and then work out what I learned from it.

I've done that with business and sometimes it doesn't work. I've been close to two infomercials and they've blown up in my face. Oh well, it was nothing, it just happened.

Now I'm lined up for my second one and it shows you've gotta keep being relentless. Don't listen to the naysayers. They're always going to tear you down. Don't listen to your family because sometimes they don't know any better.

What do you want to do? What do you want to do with your life? Who are you becoming? It's easy to know who you're not. I'm not an asshole. I can be a pain in the arse but I'm not an asshole.

I'm not a scumbag, I'm not a thief, I'm not a liar, I'm not a bullshit artist. I'm not fat. I'm in shape. I'm not out of shape. I continually push my envelope.

Know who you're not. Knowing who you are takes time and evolves over time. Take a page from Stephen Covey and his book *The Seven Habits of Highly Effective People* and do some daily self-renewal. Walk the river, walk the lake, go swimming, whatever it is, it's as simple as that.

Sit and listen to music. Sit and listen to music in the shower.

Companionship is a great gift, as is being okay with yourself. And don't buy everything the fucking lab coats tell you. There's always an alternative, always a way.

Why do people train, why do people exercise? It makes you feel better and gets rid of the bad crap.

Most diseases in nature are called hypokinetic — lack of activity. Guess what? Be active.

But in this society, what have we become? We're not chopping wood anymore, we're not chopping trees, we're not tending gardens, we're not mowing lawns, we're not doing any of that because it's all plug and play.

Go out there and bust your ass.

Years ago, we used to burn 1400 calories, just looking for food and now we cook food, we Uber food.

Get off your ass. Get off your ass and just do it. Like Nike said *Just do it*. I say just do it now.

And if you don't have an hour to exercise, don't fall into the trap of not having that hour all the time. Make time. No excuses.

You may only have 20 minutes or maybe even just 10 minutes but the key is starting. You have to start somewhere. The journey of a thousand miles starts with one step. One step towards greatness and remember that you are greatness.

You are greatness, keep telling yourself that. Write down the positive words you like and remember them. Put them in your mental rolodex.

You are relentless, you are great, you will be somebody and you are somebody. The fact that you're here is enough to tell you that you matter. The fact that you're here is enough to tell you that you matter. You matter. It doesn't matter what anybody else says. It doesn't matter what your family says, it doesn't matter what society says, I don't give a fuck.

Fuck what they say, man. You're here, you're breathing. Find that thread, hold onto that thread and keep moving forward.